Marx and Critical Theory

Critical Theory

Volumes published in this Brill Research Perspectives title are listed at *brill.com/rpct*

Marx and Critical Theory

By

Emmanuel Renault

BRILL

LEIDEN | BOSTON

This paperback book edition is simultaneously published as issue 2.1 (2017) of *Critical Theory*, DOI:10.1163/24519529-12340003.

Library of Congress Control Number: 2018944453

Typeface for the Latin, Greek, and Cyrillic scripts: "Brill". See and download: brill.com/brill-typeface.

ISBN 978-90-04-37493-5 (paperback)
ISBN 978-90-04-37494-2 (e-book)

Published by Koninklijke Brill NV, Leiden, The Netherlands.
Koninklijke Brill NV incorporates the imprints Brill, Brill Hes & De Graaf, Brill Nijhoff, Brill Rodopi, Brill Sense and Hotei Publishing.

Contents

Marx and Critical Theory

Emmanuel Renault
Professor of Social and Political Philosophy, Université Paris Nanterre
emmanuel.renault@wanadoo.fr

Abstract

Marx and Critical Theory examines Marx's main philosophical, political and social theoretical ideas. Its purpose is twofold: making sense of the concepts and theses of Marx, and showing that they remain relevant for contemporary critical theory. Part 1 focuses on Marx's conception of philosophy. Part 2 analyses the Marxian primacy of the practical. Part 3 is devoted to *Capital* and the critique of political economy. This book will be useful for those who want to deepen their understanding of Marx's main ideas, as well as for those who want to clarify what is at stake in contemporary debates about the ways in which contemporary critical theory could or should refer to Marx.

Keywords

Marx – Dewey – Foucault – Adorno – critical theory – critique of political economy – philosophy – practical turn – alienation – domination – critique – materialism – dialectics – presentism

Introduction

Marx and Freud are probably the two authors whose influence on contemporary culture has been the most pervasive. In ordinary language, concepts such as 'exploitation', 'classes', and 'capitalism' are often used in their Marxian senses, and it is often that people speak of 'subconscious', 'repression' or 'neurosis' in the Freudian sense of these terms. But Marx's influences on the various branches of contemporary critical theory are both deeper and more conscious, even if there is a tendency in contemporary critical theory to elaborate criticisms of Marx rather than making explicit what is inherited from Marx. In this introduction, it could then be useful to start with an overview of these multifarious inheritances, setting aside those who still define themselves

 | DOI:10.1163/9789004374942_002

as Marxists (for instance F. Jameson or Žižek) or Post-Marxists (Laclau and Mouffe, or Balibar) and who are generally reluctant to think of themselves as belonging to the tradition of critical theory.

To begin, let's recall that the deep influence exerted by Marx on the critical theory of the Frankfurt School goes without saying. The program of the first generation of the Frankfurt critical theory was mainly to draw on Hegel to support Marx's philosophical views and to use Freudian and Weberian concepts and theses in order to re-actualize his social theory.[1] The influence of Marx on the second and third generation of Frankfurt school has surely been less obvious and direct, but it remains decisive. The main author of the second generation, J. Habermas, elaborated his main book, *Theory of Communicative Action*, at a time when he was also working on a *Reconstruction of Historical Materialism*.[2] The main author of third generation, A. Honneth, has even more clearly connected his theoretical contribution with concepts of Marxian origin, such as 'ideology' or 'reification'.[3]

In other branches of contemporary critical theory, the inheritance of Marx was also obvious at their beginnings. This is the case in the Cultural-studies and the Subaltern-studies, who initially conceived themselves as Marxist research programs deeply influence by Gramsci's theory of culture and of subaltern groups.[4] In Foucauldian critical theory, the inheritance of Marx is also not in doubt. Foucault used Marx's analysis of the 'Factory Discipline' in *Discipline and Punish*, and more generally, he depicted Marx's *Capital* as a model for the analysis of power relations in their technical and institutional dimensions, as well as with their imbrication with the resistances they evoke.[5] It is striking that Cultural-studies, Subaltern-studies and Foucaldian critical theory, while initially consisting of research programs inspired as least in some respect by Marx, are now commonly identified as alternatives to Marx. The introduction is not the place to enter into an analysis of the historical and ideological factors that have contributed to such a reversal. I will content myself with recalling

1 See R. Wiggershaus, *The Frankfurt School: Its history, theories and political significance*, Cambridge, MA: MIT Press, 1994.

2 J. Habermas, "Towards a Reconstruction of Historical Materialism", *Theory and Society*, Vol. 2, No. 3. (Autumn, 1975), 287–300.

3 On the Marxian horizon of Honneth's writtings, see J.-P. Deranty, *Beyond Communication. A critical study of Honneth's social philosophy*, Leiden: Brill, 2009.

4 See R. Williams, *Marxism and Literature*, Oxford: Oxford University Press, 1977, Ch. 6 and D. Arnold, "Gramsci and peasant subalternity in India", *The Journal of Peasant Studies*, Volume 11, Issue 4, 1984, 155–177.

5 M. Foucault, "The Meshes of Power", in *Space, Knowledge and Power: Foucault and geography*, edited by Jeremy W. Crampton and Stuart Elden, Aldershot: Ashgate, 2007, ch. 16.

that Deleuze and Derrida, who were the contemporaries of the beginnings of such a reversal and who were also aware that they were used, just as Foucault who had already passed away, to justify a general, undifferentiated and superficial rejection of Marx, have tried to struggle against such a reversal. Derrida published *Specters of Marx* in 1993.[6] Deleuze died in 1995 before having finished (and maybe not having even really started) the book project on Marx he had planned.[7]

The same can be said of Feminist critical theory. Here again, Marx's inheritance should not be underestimated, even if less direct and general. There is no doubt that Marx is not a feminist thinker and that he did not think of domestic labour as exploited labor.[8] It remains, though, that some 'materialist feminists' have drawn on Marx to think of male domination in term of 'sexual division of labour' and in terms of exploitation of domestic labour. In other strands of Feminism, Marxian concepts and theses could also play a decisive role, for instance in J. Butler who draws on Althusser's theory of ideology and Adorno's conception of reification and alienation.[9]

In what follows, I will focus on what I consider the dimensions of Marx's thought that have produced the most enduring effects on the various traditions of critical theory. I will consider three central themes: the deflationary definition of philosophy (part 1), the materialist conception of practice and history (part 2), and the project of a critique of political economy (part 3). Each of these themes has had multiples effects on philosophy, political theory and social science in 20th and 21th centuries, and not only in the sectors which think of themselves as elaborating critical theories. Describing all of these effects is not the objective of these parts which will only try to make sense of some concepts and theses and help in understanding why they have been so influential. In other words, these concepts and theses will be considered for themselves, or from a Marxian perspective, and not from the point of view of their use in contemporary in critical theory to which I will refer only occasionally.

---

6 J. Derrida, *Specters of Marx: The State of the Debt, The Work of Mourning & the New International*, New York: Routledge, 1994.

7 The best synthesis concerning Deleuze's relation to Marx is G. Sibertin-Blanc, *Politics and State. Deleuze and Guattari on Marx*, Cambridge, MA: MIT Press, 2016.

8 For a synthesis, see F. Haug, "Marx withing Feminism", http://www.friggahaug.inkrit.de/documents/marxinfem.pdf.

9 J. Butler, *The Psychic Life of Power*, Standford: Stanford University Press, 1997; J. Butler, *Giving an Account of Oneself*, New York: Fordham University Press, 2005.

The following parts will focus on Marx himself and on interpretative debates, but these debates are too numerous to be systematically taken into account. Each phase of the history of Marxism, just as each phase of the development of critical theory, has given rise to new interpretations of Marx. There is no doubt that this remark applies to the type of reading of Marx that is proposed in the following parts: it is belonging to our time, and to the current state of the debates in critical theory. As we shall see in the first part, the issue of the Marxian status of philosophy cannot be raised today in the same way as when Marxism was not only an option for critical theory, but also a political force about to take political power in many countries. We will also see in the second part that the practice turn is one of the trademark philosophical debates of the 20th and 21th centuries and helps in reading the thesis of the unity of theory and practice in renewed ways. And finally, we'll see in the third part that the contemporary debates in social theory helps in disclosing the unexpected complexity and accuracy in *Capital*. But in the following parts, the focus will be on Marx's writings rather than on their reception or the historicity of their interpretation. At the end of this introduction, I must also make clear that this is mainly in the perspective of one specific strand of critical theory that this book is written, namely Frankfurt critical theory. That is the reason why the conclusion of this book will analyze the various uses of Marx in the various phases of the development of this type of critical theory and will call for a stronger alliance with Marx.

Part 1: Philosophy

Marx has not been influential only because of the concepts he has elaborated and the theses he has supported, but also because of his form of theorizing. He is usually considered as one of the great names in the history of philosophy and one of the founders of the social sciences. But he can also be considered as one of those who criticized the traditional status of philosophy, and it is simply a fact that he devoted a great part of his intellectual life to the critique of the main, if not the unique, social science of his time, namely political economy. These two criticisms deserve consideration. In fact, if Marx remains our contemporary, 200 years after his birth, it is notably because he is partly responsible, just as Nietzsche, Freud, Dewey, Wittgenstein and Heidegger, for the fact that it does not seem possible, nowadays, to practice philosophy as at the time of Aristotle, Descartes or Kant. Conversely, Marx did not believe that philosophy could be simply replaced by social sciences. He did not substitute philosophy with political economy but with critique of political economy. Now, many methodological features of his critique of political economy seem to be of philosophical origin: the reflection on the ontological and methodological assumptions of criticized theories and the critical analysis of the logical content of the main concepts used in these theories. Undisputedly, he believed that philosophical discourse would lose all of its value if it was not strongly connected to empirical inquiries and theories grounded in empirical inquiries, but this led him to elaborate some kind of critical social science (his critique of political economy) in which some methods and aims of the social sciences are coupled with some methods and aims of a philosophical nature. In this first part, I will focus on Marx's relation to philosophy, postponing the discussion of his critique of political economy to part 3.

The question of the status of philosophy in Marx is one of the questions that provides illustration to a point made in the introduction: Marx cannot be read today in the same manner as one hundred years ago. In the golden years of Marxism as a political force, this question has generally been posed in a form that depended on the unification of the trade unions and the masses around a worldview to which this philosophy would give its articulation as well as its foundation. Moreover, Marxist philosophy was supposed to demonstrate the superiority of the materialist science of history over any empirical study of society. Today, after the institutional crisis of the labor movement, the diversification of struggles against domination and the development of specialized knowledge about society, the traditional Marxist division of labor, which reserves philosophy with the task of founding a worldview and defending the superiority of a materialist science of history over any other knowledge, may appear anachronistic. The debate over philosophy seems to have been displaced. Rather than orchestrating the themes of the alliance of philosophy with the proletariat ("Contribution to the critique of Hegel's philosophy of Law. Introduction") or the unity of philosophy with the positive sciences (*Economic and Philosophic Manuscripts of 1844*), it seems more fruitful for contemporary critical theory to recall the ways in which Marx has claimed that philosophy should abandon its aspirations to autonomy and sovereignty over knowledges and practices, while learning from the positive knowledge of history and society and reflectively participating in struggles aimed at emancipation.

In what follows, I begin by recalling the classical terms of the problem of philosophy in Marx before depicting him as the promotor of a new practice of philosophy and, finally, arguing in favor of a deflationary conception of philosophy (that is, purged of its excessive pretensions), the interest and stakes of which can be more easily seen today than in the past.

The Early and the Mature Marx: Continuity or Discontinuity?

Is Marx a Philosopher? This naive question immediately leads us to a problem of periodization that has been mater of numerous discussions in the Marxisms as well as in Marx scholarship. Of course, Marx began his intellectual career by writing a thesis on *The Difference Between the Natural Philosophies of Democritus and Epicurus* (1841) in the hope of attaining a professorship in philosophy. Before *The German Ideology* (1845–1846, unpublished), he wrote many texts that are undeniably philosophical in design, for instance his *Contribution to Hegel's philosophy of Law* (1843, unpublished). But in *The German Ideology*, he began the project of 'leaving philosophy': 'one has to leap out of it and devote oneself like an ordinary man to the study of actuality.'[10]

If by 'philosophy', we merely mean a type of theoretical writing recognizable by such general criteria as self-reflection, abstract and systematic analysis, reflection on the principles and methods of knowledge, and the search for the general properties of objects of knowledge and action, then the answer is clear: around 1845–1846, Marx ceased to be a philosopher and started to become what we now call a theorist of the social sciences (economics, politics, and history) and a political intellectual. But things are obviously not so simple, on the one hand, because it is possible that the mature Marx attempted to formulate or deepen his earlier philosophical intuitions via other theoretical means, and on the other hand, because it is also legitimate to use the term 'philosophy' to describe the fundamental presuppositions and implications of non-philosophical texts (or the principles underlying worldviews).[11] Hence, the first interpretative alternative emerges.

According to one interpretation, which we might call 'continuist', Marx's philosophy is to be found in the philosophical texts of the early period, with the rest of his work merely applying the principles and methods elaborated in the early period to different objects. This is the interpretation that was most often privileged within Marxism and Critical Theory (and that can be found in authors as diverse as Engels, Plekhanov, Korsch, Lukács and Marcuse[12]).

10 K. Marx, F. Engels, *Collected Works* (quoted CW in what follows), London: Lawrence & Wishart, vol. 5, 1976, p. 236.

11 It is in this sense that Gramsci, for example, understood the idea of philosophy. See in particular A. Gramsci, *Prison Notebooks*, New York: Columbia University Press, 2010, 3.351–353.

12 F. Engels, *Ludwig Feuerbach and the End of Classical German Philosophy*, Moscow: Foreign Languages Pub. House, 1950; G.V. Plekhanov, *The Development of the Monist View of History*, Moscow: Foreign Languages Publishing House, 1956; K. Korsch, *Karl Marx*, New York: Russell & Russell, 1963; G. Lukács, *Le Jeune Marx: son évolution philosophique de 1840*

The early writings tend to be presented as a journey in the course of which Marx eventually reached his final philosophical position by combining various philosophical influences (primarily Hegel, Feuerbach, French materialism, and the Scottish Enlightenment). The early writings are hence considered as providing the philosophical basis of the mature writings.

According to a second interpretation, which might be called 'discontinuist', the mature works are characterized by a genuine break with the principles and methods developed in the early period, and it is precisely in this break with philosophy that the philosophical substance of Marx's thinking is to be found. This second interpretation remains associated with Althusser and his theory of an 'epistemological break' between the early Marx and the mature Marx.[13] Another version of the 'discontinuist' hypothesis is that Marx's mature works are characterized by a twofold break. *The German Ideology* shouldn't be conceived of as an 'epistemological break' but as a philosophical shift from Hegelian idealism and Feuerbachian naturalism to historical materialism. The epistemological break, consisting in a shift from philosophical historical materialism to an interdisciplinary science of history would occur later and be completed only in *The Capital* (1967).[14] While the first interpretation identifies the philosophy of Marx with that which is recognizable as philosophical within Marx's texts, the two versions of the second interpretation turn toward the implicit philosophy of what is not recognizable as philosophical in texts aiming to produce scientific effects (hence the idea of a 'symptomatic reading' of *Capital* in Althusser's school) or toward the implicit philosophy of the very project of 'leaving philosophy'.[15]

These two alternatives have symmetrical flaws. The first tends to underestimate the specificity of the methods and challenges of the mature texts by abstractly reducing them to unchanging principles (the critique of alienation, the dialectical method, materialism, and the primacy of the practical) and sometimes by assuming a traditional image of philosophy that the early Marx had already challenged. The second, conversely, especially in its Althusserian version, tries to account for the specificity of his mature work, but in so radically detaching it from the philosophical formulations of the early period and their occasional recurrences, it makes it highly unlikely that Marx would

---

à 1844, Paris: les Éd. de la Passion, 2002; H. Marcuse, *Reason and Revolution: Hegel and the Rise of Social Theory*, New York: Humanities Press, 1955.

13 L. Althusser, *For Marx*, London: Verso, 1990, 13.

14 U. Lindner, *Marx und die Philosophie*, Stuttgart: Schmetteling Verlag, 2013.

15 L. Althusser and É. Balibar, *Reading Capital*, trans. Ben Brewster (London: Verso, 1965/1997).

recognize as his own the philosophy that is imputed to him via this reconstruction. There is no doubt that any attempt to reconstruct Marx's philosophical position should focus on the project of 'leaving philosophy',[16] but in many respects, this project is anticipated in the Early period, notably by the critique of Hegelian idealism and of the search of a 'new principle' in Feuerbach and Ruge.[17] And the fact that the identification of philosophy to 'critique',[18] which is central in the early period, is still at play in the critique of political economy, proves that the break with philosophy has never been so radical.

Then, what is Marx's philosophy? This question can again be understood in two different ways: it simultaneously concerns the *philosophical status* of his theory and the nature of his *philosophical position*. As to the status of philosophy, in acknowledgement that Marx has not simply 'leapt out of philosophy', the question is whether Marx only proposed a new practice of philosophy or whether he elaborated a new philosophy. These issues have been tackled in many ways in Marxism and Marx scholarship. The first interpretations of Marx's theory as a *new philosophy* date to the period in which Marxism was being disseminated and systematized by authors such as G. Plekhanov and A. Labriola.[19] In the work of Kautsky, in particular, an opposing tendency developed, inspired by some of Engels' formulations, in which philosophy was reduced to a *reflection on the findings of the sciences*. It is in reaction against the scientism and evolutionism of the Second International and the political quietism that accompanied it that K. Korsch and others sought to rehabilitate the critical function Marx assigned to philosophy.[20] With the same intention, authors such as G. Lukács and E. Bloch[21] sought to clarify what was at stake in Marx as they elaborated their own philosophical positions. Subsequently, it was against some kind of *abrogation* of philosophy by the dogmatism of the

16 The approach consisting of interpreting the philosophical content of Marx's project starting from the idea of 'leaving philosophy' is notably that of G. Labica, *Marxism and the Status of Philosophy*, Sussex, UK: Harvester Press, 1980, and D. Brudney, *Marx's Attempt to Leave Philosophy*, Cambridge, MA: Harvard University Press, 1998.

17 See Marx's letter to A. Ruge dated September 1843 and reproduced in the introduction of the *Deutsch-Französisch Jahrbücher*; CW 3, 144.

18 See E. Renault, *Marx et l'idée de critique*, Paris: Puf, 1995, and *Marx et la philosophie*, Paris: Puf, 2014.

19 G. Plekhanov, *The Development of the Monist View of History*; A. Labriola, *Essays on the Materialistic Conception of History*, New York: Monthly Review Press, 1966.

20 K. Korsch, *Marxism and Philosophy*, New York: Monthly Review Press, 1971.

21 G. Lukács, *History and Class Consciousness: Studies in Marxist Dialectics*, Cambridge, MA: MIT Press, 1971; E. Bloch, *The Principle of Hope*, Cambridge, MA: MIT Press, 1986.

Third International, and its so called *diamat* (dialectical materialism) that a writer such as Adorno defended philosophy as a means of ethical, political and epistemological resistance.[22] But Adorno could also be referred to as a third line of interpretation, traced by the founders of the Frankfurt School[23] and Althusser,[24] according to which Marx's theoretical contributions helped define a *new practice* of philosophy rather than a new philosophy, or a reduction of philosophy to a methodology, or a rejection of philosophy.

What is at stake in these interpretative debates about the status of philosophy in Marx concerns far reaching issues that the Marxist discussions have contributed to articulate. What is the status of philosophy in a period when metaphysics can no longer be considered as the 'queen of sciences'? How should we conceive of the relationships between philosophy and the social sciences when the latter have emancipated themselves from philosophy? How should we think of the interconnections between political practices and the social criticism articulated by philosophers? How should we conceive the embeddedness of philosophical theories in their historical contexts? These questions, which are constitutive of what has been termed the 'philosophical discourse of modernity' by Habermas,[25] should probably be traced back to Hegel and Young Hegelianism, as suggested by Habermas, and leaves no doubt that Marx inherited these questions from Hegel when he was still a Young Hegelian. But in his mature period, Marx also introduced many philosophical themes that have made it possible to articulate more precisely these questions, and to investigate further their various sociological, epistemological and political implications. His views about dialectics, materialism, and philosophy of practice can therefore be considered in a twofold perspective: as defining Marx's philosophical position and as belonging to Marx's reflection about the necessity of transforming the practices of philosophy. In what follows, I would like to suggest that this second perspective is less problematic and more fruitful than the first one.

---

22 See for example, T.W. Adorno, "Why Still Philosophy?", *Critical Models: Interventions and Catchwords*, New York: Columbia University Press, 1998, 5–18.

23 See H. Marcuse, "Philosophy and Critical Theory", *Negations: Essays in Critical Theory*, Boston: Beacon Press, 1968, 134–158.

24 L. Althusser, *Lenin and Philosophy, and Other Essays*, New York: Monthly Review Press, 1972.

25 J. Habermas, *The Philosophical Discourse of Modernity: Twelve Lectures*, Cambridge, MA: MIT Press, 1985.

New Philosophy or New Practice of Philosophy?

To avoid having to postulate either an image of philosophy that Marx would have contested or a set of philosophical principles that he would not have recognized as his own, one must take as a point of departure Marx's explicitly philosophical period that is Young Hegelianism, and the questions that he explicitly addressed then: how can theory contribute to raising his contemporaries' awareness of their own interests? How can it contribute to a critique of the social situation that makes it impossible for these interests to be satisfied? How can one critique the inadequate forms of consciousness that stand in the way of a transformation of this reality? It is simply a fact that even after his attempts to 'leave philosophy', Marx's conception of theoretical activity was still oriented by these very questions that call for interconnection of knowledge, self-reflection and criticism. Now such interconnections are in a way typically philosophical. This suggests that Marx has been led to define a new practice of philosophy rather than a new philosophy or a rejection of all types of philosophical intentions and methods; a new practice of philosophy that is still at work in his historical and political writings of the later period (for instance, *The Civil War in France*, 1871) as well as in his critique of political economy.

It is not surprising that the division of intellectual labor has most often led philosophers to believe that their special task was to defend the philosophical value of Marx's work by interpreting it as having a profound and original philosophical value. To do so, they had two options: either to seek to identify the core of Marx's philosophical innovations on its own terms or to measure its originality by comparing it with other figures in philosophy. In both cases, interpretative conflicts abounded. For some, Marx's philosophy was fundamentally Spinozist,[26] while others drew comparisons with Kant,[27] Hegel[28] or Schelling.[29] According to others, the philosophical greatness of

---

26 The Spinozist interpretation of Marx was developed by Althusser and his students in a controversy with Hegelian interpretations of Marx (see for example, P. Macherey, *Hegel or Spinoza*, Minneapolis: University of Minnesota Press, 2011).

27 The first Kantian interpretations of Marx were developed at the turn of the 19th and 20th centuries in the orbit of Neo-Kantianism with authors such as Eduard Bernstein and Max Adler (see the collection edited by H.-J. Sandkühler and R. de la Vega, *Marxismus und Ethik: Texte zum neukantianischen Sozialismus*, Frankfurt: Suhrkamp, 1974).

28 Hegelian interpretations of Marx are mainly associated with the critical Marxism of Lukács and Korsch and their continuation in the Frankfurt School (see for example Herbert Marcuse, *Reason and Revolution*).

29 See M. Frank, *Der unendliche Mangel an Sein: Schellings Hegelkritik und die Anfänge der Marxschen Dialektik*, Munich: W. Fink Verlag, 1992, and "Schelling's Critique of Hegel and the Beginnings of Marxian Dialectics", *Idealistic Studies*, Volume 3, 2010: 251–268.

Marx inhabited his redefinition of materialism[30] or in the invention of a 'praxis philosophy',[31] while others instead ascribed him with the merit of having invented a new dialectic,[32] and still others celebrated the originality of his epistemology (his socio-historical redefinition of knowledge and science[33]).

Marx's work is diverse and aporetic, and multiple approaches are possible. The famous materialist, dialectical, rationalist, Spinozian, Kantian, Hegelian, and Schellingian interpretations have, at any rate, proved their fecundity. However, it is reasonable to ask whether these interpretations do not miss a fundamental characteristic of Marx's theoretical work, highlighted in particular by the Derridean interpretation of the dissemination of the philosophical *logos*.[34] Marx questioned the very forms of philosophical activity and hence paved the way to deconstructionist approaches to philosophy. The problem with interpretations that compare Marx to some of the greatest names in the history of philosophy is that they assume, if only implicitly, that Marx's philosophy is consistent with the classical image of a system based on a founding principle. This problem is shared with the interpretations that are looking for the philosophical principle of Marx's writings (materialism? dialectics? practice?). In seeking to identify the philosophical content using a classical model of philosophical activity, these interpretations do not take seriously enough the

30 One could trace this option back to the interpretation of the history of philosophy opposing in an idealist camp and a materialist camp in Engels' *Ludwig Feuerbach*, rather than to the manner in which Plekhanov and Lenin (*Materialism and Empiriocriticism*, Peking: Foreign Languages Press, 1972) attempted to clarify the nature of Marx's materialism.

31 The interpretation of Marxism as a philosophy of praxis can be traced to Labriola and Gramsci. J.-P. Sartre in his *Critique of Dialectical Reason*, London: NLB, 1976, Lukács, and Bloch constitute other sources of inspiration for writers who today adhere to a philosophy of praxis.

32 Engels tried to articulate the dialectical framework of Marx's theories while extending it to the philosophy of nature (in the texts posthumously published under the title of *Dialectics of Nature* in 1935/1940). Dialectical interpretations reappeared in the work of critics of the Second International's scientism such as Lukács and Korsch. For recent dialectical interpretations, see B. Ollman and T. Smith (eds), *Dialectics for the New Century*, Basingstoke, UK: Palgrave Macmillan, 2008.

33 Althusser and G. Della Volpe (*Logic as a Positive Science*, London: NLB, 1980) are without doubt among the main interpreters of Marx who have given more importance to the question of Marxist epistemology.

34 J. Derrida, *Specters of Marx*; "Marx & Sons", in *Ghostly Demarcations: A Symposium on Jacques Derrida's Specters of Marx*, edited by M. Sprinker, London: Verso, 1999, 213–269.

hypothesis that Marx developed his critique of philosophy in the name of a new conception of philosophy, namely a deflationary conception of philosophy.

While Marx began (under Hegelian inspiration) by presupposing a maximalist conception of philosophy as a science and had even claimed in the *Manuscripts of 1844* (under Feuerbachian inspiration) the traditional philosophical project of a knowledge that would encompass and unify philosophy and science,[35] he finally rejected philosophy's aspiration to autonomy and retained of it only the specific methodological instruments of self-reflection, synthesis, and critical analysis, bringing these to bear on other discourses (mainly that of political economy) and even on the practices of class struggle. Abandoning the illusory pretensions of philosophy to establish itself as a hegemonic knowledge, transforming it in order to avoid the negative consequences of philosophical maximalism on the understanding of the world and social critique, and finally, reducing philosophy to its fundamental theoretical operations (methodological reflexivity, synthesis of general knowledge, and critical function) while closely associating these with the dynamics of positive science and social practice: these operations all belong to a deflationary conception of philosophy. Marx can, in this sense, be reconciled with the transformations that have deeply influenced the philosophical discussion in the 20th century, notably the transformations of philosophy proposed by Dewey (under the concept of a 'reconstruction of philosophy') and the founders of the Frankfurt School (under the concept of 'critical theory'). Unlike other deflationary conceptions of philosophy (such as those inspired by Wittgenstein[36]), they were not content to assign philosophy a merely therapeutic role (or that of a criticism of the dead ends of the traditional form of philosophical activity); they also assigned it the tasks of generalization and practical intervention. In comparing Marx with Dewey and the Frankfurt School, I am neither trying to locate the heart of Marx's philosophy in the work of other philosophers nor asserting a general conformity between heterogeneous theoretical projects, but I am only trying to explain what is *at issue* for a certain kind of *practice of philosophy*.

Many points of agreement can be found between Marx's philosophical orientation and Dewey's pragmatism. In the latter, the term 'pragmatism' denotes an attempt to fight against philosophical dualisms on behalf of the primacy of practice (with the suspicion that these dualisms express class

35 CW3, 304: 'Natural science will in time incorporate into itself the science of man, just as the science of man will incorporate into itself natural science: there will be one science'.

36 See for instance R. Rorty, *Contingency, Irony and Solidarity*, Cambridge: Cambridge University Press, 1989.

divisions).[37] Dewey demands, first, that philosophy retains of its traditional ambitions only what remains tenable in light of the progress of the natural sciences and the transformations of culture and society,[38] and secondly, that it should actively intervene in practical conflicts in order to contribute effectively to social progress.[39] Just as Dewey defines his perspective as naturalist and humanist[40] and draws on an anthropology similar to that of Marx in the *Manuscripts of 1844*, so too Dewey fundamentally interprets practice as a process of self-transformation and transformation of the environment.[41] Like Marx in the *Theses on Feuerbach* and *The German Ideology*, he demands that philosophy adopt the principle of the primacy of the social,[42] to the point that the capacity of a theory to effectively fight against forms of class and gender domination become criteria of its validity.[43] The normative perspectives of Marx and Dewey are also comparable, insofar as the latter argues that politics takes priority over morals and evaluates institutions in terms of their ability to satisfy fundamental interests and liberate capacities for action that are otherwise hindered.[44] This in a manner that is comparable with the Spinozist horizon of some Marxian statements. Indeed, in the context of the 'Cold War' after World War II, a comparison of Marx's main philosophical orientations with American pragmatism would have appeared as highly counter-intuitive. It would also have appeared misleading to connect Dewey with critical theory, given the very unfavorable assessments of Horkheimer and Marcuse. But it now seems obvious

37 See for example, J. Dewey, *Reconstruction in Philosophy*, New York: Henry Holt and Co., 1920, 32, 126. In *Art as Experience* (New York: Perigee Books, 2005), 25–26, 99–100) Dewey explicitly relates the distinction between official art and popular art, and the distinction between art and work, to class prejudices. The first pragmatist interpretation of Marx can be found in the contributions of the young S. Hook (http://www.marxists.org/history/etol/writers/hook/) and his *Towards the Understanding of Karl Marx, A Revolutionary Interpretation*, New York: John Day Co., 1933; see, in this regard, C. Phelps, *Young Sidney Hook: Marxist and Pragmatist*, Ithaca, NY: Cornell University Press, 1997.

38 This is the general theme of *Reconstruction in Philosophy*.

39 See for example J. Dewey, "The Influence of Darwin on Philosophy", in *The Influence of Darwin on Philosophy and Other Essays*, New York: Henry Holt and Co., 1910, 17: 'Philosophy must in time become a method of locating and interpreting the more serious of the conflicts that occur in life, and a method of projecting ways for dealing with them; a method of moral and political diagnosis and prognosis.' See also *Reconstruction in Philosophy*, ch. 8.

40 J. Dewey, *Experience and Nature*, New York: George Allen Unwin, 1929.

41 J. Dewey, *Democracy and Education: An Introduction to the Philosophy of Education*, New York: Macmillan, 1916, chapter 8.

42 J. Dewey, "The Social as a Category", *Monist* 38 (April 1928), 161–177.

43 J. Dewey, *Reconstruction in Philosophy*, 125.

44 See J. Dewey, *Reconstruction in Philosophy*, ch. 8.

that the Marxian and Frankfurtian harsh criticisms of Dewey were dependent on a relative ignorance of the specific positions held by Dewey, whom Adorno, on his part, did not hesitate to call 'unique and truly free.'[45] In the beginning of the 21th century, it has become easier to recall that S. Hook, who was Dewey's assistant and friend, is the author of one of the first genuinely philosophical books written on Marx.[46] It has also become possible to take seriously the fact that Dewey probably exerted more influence on Mao than James on Sorel and Gramsci.[47] Many dimensions of Marx's thinking are in tune with the instrumentalist, pluralist and experimentalist orientations of Dewey's pragmatism. The criticism of dogmatism, the importance given by Marx to 'worker's inquiry', to political experiments such as *La Commune*, or to the analysis of the variety of class interests and possible alliances can be mentioned in this respect, as well as the necessity to interconnect theory and practice with regard to the specificities of changing historical situations. In other words, the deflationary conception of philosophy is not the only pragmatist element of Marx's thinking that could inspire contemporary critical theory.

But the Frankfurt critical theory can also shed light on dimensions of Marx's thought that are at odds with the pragmatist deflationary conception of philosophy. Where Dewey merely required philosophy to actively participate in social inquiry into the nature, causes, and remedies for social problems and to expose all the inadequate conceptions that impeded their practical resolution,[48] the Frankfurt School authors proposed a more radical reform of philosophy. The way in which Horkheimer opposed 'critical theory' to 'traditional theory' implies that philosophers must consider the social position they occupy and the political effects of their discourse,[49] and that specifically philosophical

45 T.W. Adorno, *Aesthetic Theory*, New York: Continuum, 2004, 426. Meanwhile, recent developments in critical theory have explicitly drawn on the pragmatism of Pierce, Dewey and Mead; see J. Habermas, *Knowledge and Human Interests*, Boston, MA: Beacon Press, 1971, and *The Theory of Communicative Action*, Boston, MA: Beacon Press, 1984; A. Honneth, *The Struggle for Recognition: The Moral Grammar of Social Conflicts*, trans. Joel Anderson, Cambridge, UK: Polity Press, 1995. On the twofold Marxist and pragmatist horizon of the latter, see Jean-Philippe Deranty, *Beyond Communication*.

46 S. Hook, *Toward the Understanding of Marx*.

47 See E. Renault, "Dewey, Hook, and Mao: on some affinities between Marxism and pragmatism", http://www.cairn-int.info/article-E_AMX_054_0137--dewey-hook-mao-on-some-affinities.htm.

48 See J. Dewey, *The Public and its Problems*, London: Allen & Unwin, 1926.

49 M. Horkheimer, "Traditional and Critical Theory", in *Critical Theory: Selected Essays*, New York: Herder and Herder, 1972, 188–243.

procedures must be transformed in order to be combined with specialized inquiries led by social and human sciences (economics, sociology, and psychology) as part of an interdisciplinary project. The project of a critical theory of society presupposes that political philosophy becomes a 'social philosophy'[50] in order to integrate itself into this interdisciplinary project; a social philosophy that in turn presents three inseparable branches: a social ontology of capitalism as a totality of mediations and contradictions, a social theory of the structures and tendencies that shape the various layers of social life, and an epistemology of human sciences.[51] If pragmatism can help articulate the philosophical implications of Max's primacy of practice, which we will investigate in the second part, Horkheimer and Adorno have tried to elaborate a dialectical conception of society and a conception of philosophy as criticism of society, ideology, and social sciences that is just as decisive in Marx's deflationary conception of philosophy, as we will see in the third part.

Without doubt, it is the Frankfurt project of a critical theory of society that best explains the challenges of the new practice of philosophy that are inscribed in Marx's critique of political economy. In Marx, the therapeutic role of the critique of philosophy, religion, and politics is finally inseparable from the effort to engage philosophers in the specialized field of political economy, while justifying this intervention from an epistemological point of view (in the context of a reflection on the 'method of political economy'[52]), in terms of a social ontology of capitalism (as a society specified by particular forms of contradictions, social mediations and processes), and in terms of a theory of the principles of social evolution (as determined by the specification of the principles of the materialist conception of history). And we will see that far from leading back to a philosophical imperialism in the guise of a new philosophy of history, the materialist conception of history is presented by Marx as a guiding thread for empirical research, and an instrument for the communist movement to reflect on the orientation of its political practice by reconstructing the historical context of its emergence. *Capital* instantiates Marx's attempt to the think of the specificity of the historical dynamics of a particular social

50 M. Horkheimer, "The State of Contemporary Social Philosophy and the Tasks of an Institute for Social Research", in *Critical Theory and Society: A Reader*, edited by. S.E. Bronner and D.M. Kellner, New York: Routledge, 1989, 25–36.

51 These three branches are conceived as definitory of the project of a 'social theory' as it is supported by Adorno in his contributions to T.W. Adorno and K. Popper, *The Positivist Dispute in German Sociology*, London: Heinemann, 1976.

52 CW 28, 37–44.

formation (the capitalist societies) and associate scientific knowledge of the present with sociological and political self-reflection.

Criticism, Materialism, Dialectics, Practice and Presentism

What is gained by replacing a maximalist conception of philosophy with such a deflationary conception? It enables philosophy to fulfill its aspirations to rational knowledge and emancipatory criticism. To retain its worth as a form of rational discourse, it must stop believing that it embodies the highest form of rationality and redefine its own practices in the light of the development of differentiated forms of rationality in the specialized sciences and in social practices. In other words, it must substitute a conception of philosophy as autonomous thought with a conception of philosophy as heteronomous thought or as a connection of 'philosophy' with that which is 'unphilosophical'.[53] Critique is Marx's concept for capturing this heteronomy of philosophical thought: philosophy as critique of political economy on the one hand and criticism of religion, criticism of politics, and criticism of utopian socialism on the other.[54] Philosophy cannot produce knowledge and social criticism but as self-reflection on empirical knowledges as well as critical reflection on social forms of consciousness, with this critical reflection being sometime denoted by the Feuerbachian term 'reform of the consciousness' in the early Marx:

> Nothing prevents us from making criticism of politics, participation in politics and therefore real struggles, the starting point of our criticism with them. In that case we do not confront the world in a doctrinary way with a new principle: Here is the truth, kneel down before it! We develop the new principles for the world out of the world's own principle. We do not say to the world: Cease your struggles, they are foolish; we will give you the true slogan of struggle. We merely show the world what it is really

53 L. Feuerbach, *Provisional Theses for the Reformation of Philosophy*, § 45: 'The philosopher must consider what in the human being does not philosophize, but rather is at odds with philosophy and opposed to abstract thinking. Thus the philosopher must bring into the text of philosophy what Hegel relegated to mere remarks. Only in this way will philosophy be irrefutable and uncontested, a universal and irresistible power. Genuine philosophy thus has to begin not with itself, but with its antithesis, with what is not philosophy. This unphilosophical, absolutely antischolastic essence in us, distinguished from thinking, is the principle of sensualism'.

54 E. Renault, *Marx et l'idée de critique*.

> fighting for, and consciousness is something it has to acquire, even if it does not want to.
>
> The reform of consciousness consists only in making the world aware of its own consciousness (...). In short, therefore, we can formulate the trend of our journal as being: self-clarification (critical philosophy) to be gained by the present time of its struggles and desires.[55]

To retain its worth as a form of rational discourse, philosophy must also renounce thinking of itself in terms of presuppositionlessness of pure thought[56] and instead, it must subject its own historical conditions and its embeddedness in the process of social life to self-reflection. In other words, it must substitute a materialist conception philosophy to an idealist one, or more precisely, it must back its conception of philosophy on a materialism conceived as a criticism of idealist assumptions of the autonomy of thought and the will. One of the distinctive characteristics of Marx's historical materialism is that it is a 'materialism without matter',[57] that is a materialism without ontology, a materialism that retains from the materialist traditions (or so called traditions) nothing else and nothing more than their critical dimensions (criticism of the dualism matter/spirit, criticism of teleological explanations, atheism, etc.). It is worth noting that materialism in Marx always means criticism of idealist assumptions: the materialist conception of practice, as it is elaborated in the *Theses on Feuerbach*, is nothing more than a critique of the idealist conception of practice; the materialist conception of history, as it is elaborated in *The German Ideology*, is above all a critique of idealist conceptions of history; the concept of 'materialist dialectic', as it is alluded to in the Postface of *Capital*, seems to denote the program of a critique of idealist assumptions of Hegel's dialectics.[58]

---

55 CW 3, 144–145.

56 As it is the case in B. Bauer, notably, who his criticized for this very reason in *The German Ideology*.

57 E. Balibar, *The Philosophy of Marx*, London: Verso, 1995, p. 23: 'Marx's materialism has nothing to do with a reference to matter'.

58 Adorno, among others, has highlighted the critical dimension of Marx's concept of dialectic: 'It was Marx who drew the line between historic materialism and the popular-metaphysical kind. He thus involved the former in the problematics of philosophy, leaving popular materialism to cut its dogmatic capers this side of philosophy. Since then, materialism is no longer a counter-position one may resolve to take; it is the critique of idealism in its entirety, and of the reality for which idealism opts by distorting it. Horkheimer's phrasing, "critical theory," seeks not to make materialism acceptable but to use it to make men theoretically conscious of what it is that distinguishes materialism – distinguishes

In this respect, criticism, and materialism are two of the main concepts of Marx's deflationary conception of philosophy. If Marx's conception of philosophy should be considered as dialectics, although he has not said much about dialectics and rarely used this concept,[59] it is precisely in these two senses of a critical and materialist self-reflection. From an epistemological point of view, as a 'mode of exposition', the notion of dialectics refers to the project of critical reflection on the contradictions of classical political economy. From a social theoretical point of view, the notion of dialectics denotes the contradictions of the capitalist society that doom this society to destruction. In both cases, as in Hegel's conception of dialectics, the contradictions are destructive as well as productive: the study of the contradictions of political economy makes a truer theory of capitalist economy possible, just as the structural contradictions of the capitalist society define communism as a possibility engaged in the process of its own actualization. Now, the structural contradictions of the capitalist society are not only shaping the process of social life, they are also shaping various forms of social consciousness. In the philosophical forms of social consciousness, this general contradiction takes the form of the contradiction between philosophy as the search for truth and emancipation, on the one hand, and philosophy as ideology, on the other, as we will see in the next part. For philosophy, thinking of itself as participating in the process of

---

it from amateurish explications of the world as much as from the "traditional theory" of science' (*Negative Dialectics*, New York: Routledge, 1973, 197).

59 Notably, it is worth noting that he has almost never use this notion during his Hegelian period, i.e. his Young-Hegelian period. See E. Renault, «The Early Marx and Hegel: The Young Hegelian Mediation», forthcoming in *Reassessing Marx's Social and Political Philosophy*, edited by J. Kandiyali, New York: Routledge, 2018. The dialectical interpretations of *The Capital* as numerous, but they have also been contested in many ways. Indeed, in the Postface of *Capital*, Marx sketched the program of a 'materialist' dialectics that would reverse the Hegelian concept of dialectics, but he never developed this program, and it is not clear in which sense *Capital* is dialectical. Marx himself has only said that in some section of *Capital*, he 'coquetted with the mode of expression peculiar to' Hegel (*Capital I*, London: Penguin, 1990, 103). Moreover, since Marx mentions dialectics in two distinct senses in this Postface as a dialectics of knowledge (or 'mode of presentation' of the critique of political economy) and as a dialectics of reality (as 'the movement of capitalist society is full of contradictions') (*ibidem*, 102, 103), one can wonder if Marx had a clear concept of dialectics at that time. As noted by Adorno, in the "Introduction" to *The Positivist Dispute*, 24: 'the possibility of devolving objective contradictions onto semantics may be connected with the fact that Marx, the dialectician, did not possess a completely developed notion of dialectics. He imagined that he was simply "flirting" with it. Thinking, which teaches itself that part of its own meaning is what, in turn, is not a thought, explodes the logic of non-contradiction.'

social life does not mean only thinking of its own historical and sociological conditions. It also means reflecting on the ways in which structural social contradiction give rise to ideological assumptions that tend to colonize the various knowledges, including philosophy. It also means that philosophy has to think of itself as the locus of a contradiction between truth and ideology, and that its rationality depends on critical reflection on this contradiction, in other words, on ideology critique.[60]

Traditionally, philosophy has not been defined only by the aspiration to rational knowledge. It also conceived of itself as a theoretical means to make the individual and social life better. And here again, in order to fulfill its ethical and political promises, philosophy has to renounce one of its traditional features. It has to renounce to its intellectualism, namely the idea that truth is the end in itself toward which philosophical theorization is oriented. It must redefine itself in order to become a theoretical means that could be useful for the human attempts to tackle the ethical and political problems they are confronted with. In other words, it must substitute a pragmatist conception of the unity of theory and practice for the spiritualist conception of theory having its end in itself. It must become what Brecht called 'intervening thought'.[61] But this requires that philosophy reflects on the specificity of the various historical contexts in which it has to intervene as a tool useful for emancipatory practices. This also means that it has to renounce its traditional self-conception concept as 'philosophia perenis', or as theory 'from the standpoint of eternity' (to use a Spinozist phrase). It has to assume a Hegelian definition of philosophy as a reflection on its own time. It has to substitute a presentism[62] for an eternitism. This presentism manifests itself notably when Marx contends that all political

---

60 Adorno has highlighted that the idea of a contradiction between truth and ideology is congenial to the Marxian concept of ideology, as contrasted with the sociological conceptions of ideology that is elaborated notably by Mannheim: 'A sociology of knowledge fails before philosophy: for the truth content of philosophy it substitutes its social function and its conditioning by interests, while refraining from a critique of that content itself, remaining indifferent toward it. It fails equally before the concept of ideology, which it will stir into its broad beggarly broth; for the concept of ideology makes sense only in relation to the truth or untruth of what it refers to. There can be no talk of socially necessary delusions except in regard to what would not be a delusion – although, of course, delusion is its index' (*Negative Dialectics*, 197).

61 B. Brecht, "Über eingreifendes Denken", in *Gesammelte Werke*, Frankfurt, Germany: Suhrkamp, 1967, 8.714–735.

62 The notion of 'presentism' has been coined as a philosophical concept by Dewey and Mead, but Hegel, who has deeply influenced Dewey and Mead, had already developed a presentist philosophy. On Hegel's presentism, see E. Renault, *Connaître ce qui est. Enquête*

programs have to take into account historical evolution (for instance in revising some of the propositions of the *Communist Manifesto* after the Parisian Commune[63]), or when he criticizes the French revolutionaries of 1848 for seeking their political models in the past (in the French Revolution), rather than elaborating the specific demands of their times.[64] The famous definition of communism, which I will analyze in the next part, also illustrates Marx's presentism: 'Communism is for us not a *state of affairs* which is to be established, an *ideal* to which reality [will] have to adjust itself. We call communism the *actual* movement which abolishes the present state of things.'[65]

When the notions of criticism, of materialism, of theory/practice unity, and of presentism are interconnected in reference to a deflationary conception of philosophy, it is mainly in the legacy of American pragmatism and in Frankfurt critical theory that Marx finds contemporary echoes. But intervening thought and presentism also echo in the Foucauldian definition of philosophy as 'ontology of the present'[66] and as the critical genealogy of powers against which social movements are actually struggling (for instance, in the connection established by Foucault between *Surveiller et Punir* and his participation in the GIP[67]). As we will see in the next part, the Marxian conception of intervening thought implies an original account of the relationships between theory and practice that finds other echoes in contemporary critical theory. Notably, the conception of theory as the self-reflection of emancipatory practices depends on a project of self-emancipation of the proletariat that found many echoes

---

sur le présentisme hégélien, Paris: Vrin, 2016. On Dewey's relations to Hegel, see E. Renault, "Dewey's Relations to Hegel", *Contemporary Pragmatism*, Volume 13, Issue 3, 219–241.

63 As highlighted, in the Preface to the 1872 German edition.

64 K. Marx, *The Eighteenth Brumaire of Louis Bonaparte* (CW 11, 154): 'The social revolution of the nineteenth century cannot take its poetry from the past but only from the future. It cannot begin with itself before it has stripped away all superstition about the past. The former revolutions required recollections of past world history in order to smother their own content. The revolution of the nineteenth century must let the dead bury their dead in order to arrive at its own content. There the phrase went beyond the content – here the content goes beyond the phrase.'

65 CW 5, 49. On Marx's presentism, see E. Renault, "Hegel, Marx, Presentism", in *From Marx to Hegel and Back Again*, edited by H. Kuch and V. Fareld, London: Bloomsbury, forthcoming in 2018.

66 See M. Foucault, "What is Enlightenment?" (1984), in *The Foucault Reader*, edited by P. Rabinow, New York: Pantheon, 1985, 32–50.

67 M. Foucault, *Discipline & Punish: The Birth of the Prison*, New York: Pantheon Books, 1977. On Foucault's activism in the Groupe Information Prison (GIP), see https://www.viewpointmag.com/2016/02/16/manifesto-of-the-groupe-dinformation-sur-les-prisons-1971/.

in Feminist conceptions of emancipation: just as the emancipation of workers cannot be achieved but by the workers, according to Marx, the emancipation of women cannot be achieved but by the women themselves, according to many Feminists who were sometimes led, as a consequence, to promote some kind of strategic 'separatism'.[68] It also echoes in Feminist 'standpoint' theories[69] in which it is highlighted that a theory has to elaborate a self-reflection on its standpoint within the various social relations of domination if it wants to really contribute to the practical struggles against a specific form of domination. This principle has been elaborated by Marx with reference to class domination, and indeed, it is relevant also for gender domination, as well as ethno-racial domination.

Part 2: Practice

Marxism is traditionally associated with the principle of the unity of theory and praxis, but this principle only expresses one of the dimensions of Marx's primacy of the practical. We will see that in the *Theses on Feuerbach*, he contends that there is an ontological as well as an epistemological primacy of the practical, and the principle of the unity of theory and practice only refers to the epistemological side of this primacy. Both sides deserve consideration.

Concerning this twofold primacy, Marx clearly follows the path of Kant, Fichte, and Hegel. Kant elaborated a conception of the primacy of the 'practical reason' over 'speculative' or theoretical reason. Fichte introduced the concept of a 'primacy of the practical'. Hegel pointed out, following Fichte, that spirit is essentially 'activity' and that its activity is engaged in a process of actualization through transformation of the external and internal nature or in actual practices of self-transformation and transformation of the environment.[70] Following Hegel, Marx tried to think of men as defined mainly by their concrete activities, activities that are always conditioned by external and internal constraints, but are also able to transform their conditions, either through work or through revolutionary action. The notion of 'practice' denotes precisely the

68 See for instance M. Frye, "Some Reflections on Separatism and Power", in *Feminist Social Thought: A Reader*, edited by D. Tietjens Meyers, New York: Routledge, 1997, 406–414.

69 For a synthesis, see T. Bowell, "Feminist Standpoint Theory", http://www.iep.utm.edu/fem-stan/.

70 I have tried to analyze the various forms of this primacy of the practical in *Connaître ce qui est. Enquête sur le présentisme hégélien*, chap. 9.

human activity conceived of in its subjective and objective conditionings as well as in its subjective and objective transformative potentials.

To begin the discussion of these themes, a terminological clarification can be useful. In German Idealism and Young Hegelianism, the primacy of the practical hasn't usually be articulated with the German word 'Praxis'. Kant referred to 'practical reason' (*praktische Vernunft*); Fichte to 'the practical' (*das Praktische*) and he pointed out that the 'I' (*Ich*) is essentially 'activity' (*Tätigkeit*) rather than substance; Hegel conceived of spirit as a series of 'activities', be they activities of the "theoretical spirit" or of the "practical spirit" (*praktischer Geist*), but he preferred to use the term 'action' (*das Tun, die Handlung*) to describe the truly spiritual practical activities (such as moral actions); Moses Hess wanted to promote a 'philosophy of the act' (*Philosophie der Tat*). None of them used the German term 'Praxis' to articulate their reflections about the primacy of the practical. Therefore, it is surely not contingent that Marx's version of the idea of a primacy of the practical is articulated with reference to 'Praxis' rather than to 'praktische Vernunft', 'das Praktische', 'die Tätigkeiten', 'die Handlung' or 'die Tat'. Indeed, in German Idealism and in Young Hegelianism, the German term 'Praxis' was already in use, but it was in another context and with another function. It was not in the context of discussions about the primacy of the practical, but about the relations between theory and its practical applications. Its function was not to enunciate an ontological or epistemological principle but to think of the status of applied science or the political application of philosophical theories of natural rights. An illustration of this latter function is provided by the famously Kantian reply to one of the arguments used against the French Revolution: 'what is true in theory is not true in praxis.'[71] Here 'Praxis' means practice in its ordinary or worldly or mundane dimensions, practice in its irreducibility to theory and also to the mere application of theory: political practices cannot be reduced to the mere application of normative principles. It is clearly in this sense that Marx speaks of 'Praxis' in the *Theses on Feuerbach*, in order to contrast an idealist conception of practice as 'subjective activity' (*subjective Tätigkeit*) or as actualisation of the freedom of the spirit or practical reason, with a materialist conception of practice as 'objective' and 'actual' (*wirklich*),[72] that is, as always conditioned by circumstances. In other words,

---

71 The argument can be phrased as follows: the philosophical theories of natural rights could be true *in abstracto*, but as soon that one tries to applied them to existing societies in order to reorganize them, they are doomed to failure.

72 'Wirklichkeit', the noun, and 'wirklich', the adjective, are notions used by Hegel to denote reality in its most concrete forms, that is as structured by relations and dynamics, or as reciprocal actions between its various moments.

the German term 'Praxis' has been selected by Marx instead of 'Tätigkeit' or 'Handlung' or 'Tat' because these terms have been associated in Fichte, Hegel and the Young Hegelians with the idealist conception of practice he was precisely criticizing.

In order to clarify the Marxian meaning of the term 'Praxis', the first three *Theses on Feuerbach* deserve special consideration. The first one highlights that in Feuerbach, as in all forms of 'old materialism', it remains impossible to understand that there is a primacy of the practical. German idealism, in Kant, Fichte and Hegel, is the true origin of the idea of the primacy of the practical, but these authors have only thought of practice as 'subjective activity', not as 'objective' or 'actual' activity. Hence, the task of the 'new materialism' Marx wants to promote is to think of the primacy of the practical with reference to practice conceived of not only as a 'subjective activity' but also as an activity conditioned subjectively (as 'sensuous human activity') and objectively (as conditioned by 'circumstances'). In the words of the second thesis, it means that new materialism thinks of practice in its 'worldliness'. And to put it in the terms used in the third thesis, it means that this new materialism criticizes the idealist conception of practice with an argument that is typical of old materialism: human activities are always conditioned by 'circumstances'. But conversely, against the old versions of materialism, Marx stresses that the circumstances can also be changed by human practices, and it is only such a potential of human practices that enables one to understand the possibility and significance of ' "revolutionary", or "practical-critical" activity'.

1. The chief defect of all previous materialism (that of Feuerbach included) is that the object (*Gegenstand*), actuality (*Wirklichkeit*), and sensuousness, are conceived only in the form of the *object* (Objekt) *of contemplation*, but not as *sensuous human activity, practice*, and not subjectively. Hence, in contradistinction to materialism, the *active* side was set forth abstractly by idealism – which, of course, does not know actual, sensuous activity as such. Feuerbach wants sensuous objects really distinct from thought objects, but he does not conceive human activity itself as *objective* activity. In *The Essence of Christianity*, he therefore regards the theoretical attitude as the only genuinely human attitude, while practice is conceived and fixed only in its dirty-Jewish form of appearance. Hence he does not grasp the significance of 'revolutionary', of 'practical-critical', activity.
2. The question whether objective truth can be attributed to human thinking is not a question of theory but is a *practical* question. Man must prove the truth, i.e., the reality and power, the this-worldliness of his thinking

in practice. The dispute over the reality or non-reality of thinking that is isolated from practice is a purely *scholastic* question.

3. The materialist doctrine concerning the changing of circumstances and upbringing forgets that circumstances are changed by men and that the educator must himself be educated. This doctrine must, therefore, divide society into two parts, one of which is superior to society. The coincidence of the changing of circumstances and of human activity or self-change can be conceived and rationally understood only as *revolutionary practice*.[73]

In these three theses, we find an illustration of one of the points made in the first part, namely that 'materialism' in Marx does not denote any theory on the primacy of 'matter' or any 'materialist ontology' but only a series of criticisms of idealist positions. There are no references to matter in the *Theses of Feuerbach*, and the materialist position elaborated in these critical notes against German idealism is nothing more than a criticism of the idealist version of the primacy of the practical. Conversely, the criticism of 'old' materialisms targets the fact that they are grounded on a theory of the 'mater' that makes it impossible to understand the nature and transformative potentials of social practices. The rest of this part is intended to elucidate the meaning and implication of this 'materialist' conception of the primacy of the practical, but before entering this discussion, a last philological remark about the German term 'Praxis' is required.

Another point suggested in the first part was that it is just as problematic to read Marx as elaborating a new materialist ontology, as to read him as promoting 'praxis' as a new philosophical principle. Those who have read Marx's texts as a 'praxis philosophy' have generally been led to think of the German term "Praxis" as a concept of high philosophical importance, inheriting the Aristotelian 'Praxis' as well as trying to overcome the Aristotelian contrast of 'Praxis' with 'Poesis'. As Aristotle, Marx would be pointing out that 'Praxis' is one of the truest human activities, but conjointly, he would refuse to consider that 'productive activities' (*Poesis*) are less human than moral and political actions (*Praxis*). Translating the German term 'Praxis' into the English term 'praxis' contributes to giving Marx's conception of practice some kind of high philosophical dignity and suggests that his conception of practice results from some kind of immanent critique of Aristotle and, more generally, of the conceptions of action elaborated in philosophical traditions. But in the *Theses on Feuerbach*, Marx is not discussing Aristotle and the philosophers who have been

73 CW 5, 3–4 (*translation modified*).

influenced by the praxis/poesis distinction; he is criticizing German Idealism and Young Hegelianism. The gist of his argument is not that practice has to be thought of in all its philosophical dignity but quite on the contrary that it must be thought of in its 'worldliness', that is in its ordinary forms with their objective and subjective conditions. A twofold conclusion results from this. The first one is that the appropriate English translation of the German 'Praxis' is 'practice' and not 'praxis'. The second one is that the philosophical implications of Marx's primacy of the practical are probably better conceived in terms of 'practice turn' than in terms of 'praxis philosophy'. Marx's philosophical intentions are probably not to promote 'practice' to a new 'first principle'. Given his deflationist conception of philosophy, it is more likely that Marx just wanted to invite us to think of society and knowledge from the point of view of their relations to practices. Here, we probably touch one of the reason why Marx is still our contemporary: his materialist account of practice is in tune with the 'practice turn' that seems so influential nowadays, not only in the philosophy of language, social theory, philosophy of mind, and of the cognitive sciences,[74] but also in contemporary critical theory.[75] In what follows, I will try to read the *Theses on Feuerbach*, the *German Ideology* and the *Communist Manifesto* as promoting a 'practice turn' in social ontology, social theory, political theory, and epistemology.

Ontological Primacy of the Practical

At the beginning of this part, I contended that Marx's conception of the primacy of the practical has two sides, one that is ontological and the other epistemological. The latter refers to the theory/practice unity to which theses 3 and 11 relate. Thesis 3 states that: 'The question whether objective truth can be attributed to human thinking is not a question of theory but is a *practical* question. Man must prove the truth, i.e., the reality and power, the this-worldliness of his thinking in practice'. In other words, the truth of theory depends on practice. According to the famous thesis 11: 'The philosophers have only *interpreted* the world in various ways; the point would be to *change* it.'[76] In other words, the critical function of theory depends on its unity with transformative

74 For an overview, see T.R. Schatzki, K. Knorr Cetina, E. von Savigny (eds), *The Practice Turn in Contemporary Theory*, New York: Routledge, 2001.

75 See for instance, R. Celikates, *Kritik als Soziale Praxis*, Frankfurt: Campus, 2009; R. Jaeggi, "A Wide Concept of Economy: Economy as a Social Practice and the Critique of Capitalism", in *Critical Theory in Critical Times*, edited by P. Deutscher, New York: Columbia University Press, 2017, ch. 8.

76 CW 5, 5.

practices. I will analyse the nature and implications of this unity of theory and practice in the next section. For the time being, let's consider the ontological dimensions of Marx's primacy of the practical.

The first interpretive problem to tackle is to decide in which sense the primacy of the practical could be considered as ontological. According to thesis 1: 'The chief defect of all previous materialism (that of Feuerbach included) is that the object, actuality, sensuousness, is conceived only in the form of the *object or of contemplation*, but not as *sensuous human activity, practice*, not subjectively.' This seems to suggest either that all reality is practical in its constitution, or that practice is the essence of all reality. But when thesis 8 states that 'all social life is essentially *practical*. All mysteries which lead theory to mysticism find their rational solution in human practice and in the comprehension of this practice',[77] it seems that Marx's point is rather that *social* reality only, and not reality in general is 'essentially practical'. Then, theses 1 and 8 are compatible with two opposite readings and the interpretative problem can be put in the following terms: does the ontological dimension of the primacy of the practical regard general ontology or only social ontology? In other words, are social entities, relations and processes the only realities that are essentially practical, or is it the case that nature also is essentially practical?

The contention, according to which all reality is by essence practical, has been attributed to Marx for instance by some of his greatest readers such as Bloch or Lukács. It is grounded on a view of nature as being a reality essentially homogeneous to society. Such a view can draw on the *Manuscripts of 1844* as well as on *The German Ideology*. In the *Manuscripts*, Marx elaborates some kind of historical naturalism according to which human activity appears as a development of natural activity, and social evolution is the highest development of natural evolution. These texts can be interpreted as having been written under a Schellingian inspiration that would remain apparent in the *Theses on Feuerbach*.[78] Just as in Schelling, nature is a productivity that becomes aware of itself in human action and intelligence, it could be said that in the *Theses on Feuerbach*, 'Praxis' denotes the moment when the natural productivity reaches its highest form. Such an interpretation is elaborated by Bloch in his reading of the *Theses on Feuerbach* in *The Principle of Hope*.[79] Another way to think of nature as being in ontological continuity with society is to highlight passages

77 CW 5, 5.

78 See M. Frank, *Der unendliche Mangel an Sein: Schellings Hegelkritik und die Anfänge der Marxschen Dialektik*, and "Schelling's Critique of Hegel and the Beginnings of Marxian Dialectics."

79 E. Bloch, *The Principle of Hope*, vol. 1, ch. 19.

of *The German Ideology* where Marx notes that what we call nature is a reality that has been transformed by its interaction with human activities. Nature is not independent from but embedded in the historical process: 'The history of nature and the history of men are dependent on each other so long as men exist.'[80] Just as society and history depends on human actions, nature is then a type of being conditioned by human actions. It is precisely from the point of view of such a kind of identification of reality with history that Lukács[81] elaborates his praxis philosophy.

In other words, there are two ways of reading Marx's philosophy as a praxis metaphysics, the first of which is naturalist, the second historicist. But each of them is questionable in many respects. Indeed, it is indisputable that there is a naturalist moment in Marx. It is the case in the Feuerbachian naturalism of 1844 as well in *The Capital*, which refers to Darwin in a quite positive way.[82] According to Marx, society is nothing but a transformation of nature through work, and it remains in relation to nature through work. That is the reason why *The Capital* defines work as some kind of organic relationship between society and nature: 'Labour is, first of all, a process between man and nature, a process by which man, through his own actions, mediates, regulates, and controls the metabolism between himself and nature.'[83] But Marx's naturalism stresses that the ontological continuity between nature and society should be conceived of as a non-reductionist or emergent naturalism.[84] He refuses to depict society only as a development of natural productivity. The specificity of social reality is linked firstly with its artificial dimension, as product of work, and secondly with its historical dimension, as product of human activity that can be transformed by human activity. Conversely, Marx refuses to reduce nature to a historical product, or as being only a moment of the historical process: nature remains external to societies and to their historical becoming. Nature is a set of material processes subjected to laws that are different from the laws of social evolution, and in each period of history, nature remains a material that has

80 CW 5, 28.

81 For a defence of such a position, and for an illustration of its legacy in the Frankfurt school, see A. Feenberg, *Philosophy of Praxis: Marx, Lukács and the Frankfurt School*, London: Verso, 2014.

82 *Capital I* (London: Penguin Classics, 1990), 493–494, note 4.

83 *Capital I*, p. 283. See also p. 132: 'Labour, then, as the creator of use-value, as useful labour, is a condition of human existence which is independent of all forms of society; it is an eternal natural necessity which mediates the metabolism between man and nature, and therefore human life itself.'

84 On the Hegelian sources of such naturalism, see E. Renault, "The Naturalist Side of Hegel's Pragmatism", *Critical Horizons*, Volume 13, Issue 2, 2012, 244–274.

to be transformed by work in order to satisfy the natural and social needs of humans, as well as to fuel socio-economic dynamics. As a consequence, nature can be thought of neither as a totality encompassing society, nor as a moment of the all-encompassing historical reality. Rather, it is a reality independent of society but always linked with it, just as society always remains linked with nature. On the one hand, society and nature remains external to each other, but on the other hand, each of them depends on the other, so that their relations are internal rather than external relations.

To put it in ontological terms, it could be said that Marx conception of reality in general is a conception of reality that is relational and dynamical: the reality of nature and society can neither be separated from the reality of their relations, nor from the reality of their specific becoming, natural evolution, and history. This leads to a conception of reality as 'reciprocal action' (*Wechselwirkung*) in the Hegelian meaning of the term, and we will see that the relation between the various moments of social life is also thought of as 'reciprocal action' by Marx. Just as there is reciprocal action between nature and society, there is reciprocal action between the economic structure of society, superstructure, and ideology. Therefore, if one would want to attribute a metaphysical position to Marx, one should claim that Marx's metaphysics or general ontology, two concepts denoting a theory of the generic characteristics of reality, is a metaphysics or general ontology of reciprocal action, not of praxis. Since Hegel depicted 'reciprocal action' as the truest of the ontological categories, those categories critically analysed in the first part of his Science of logic, the "Objective logic",[85] it could then be concluded that Marx's metaphysical position is inherited from Hegel, or that Marx's ontological commitments are part of the Hegelian deposit in his thought.

But if there is no praxis metaphysics in Marx, how should we read the first sentence of the first thesis on Feuerbach? What is the meaning of the contention according to which reality *in general* shouldn't be conceived of as theoretical 'object' but as 'praxis' if this meaning is not ontological? The only consistent answer is that this contention has a phenomenological rather than ontological meaning: this contention doesn't relate to the features of reality as such but of reality as it is given to us. Reality is not given to us primarily as a series of objects cognized or objects of theorization, but as factors of our actions, as possibilities to acts or as possible obstacles to overcome. Our information about the external world is primarily sensitive information, and the sensitive information we are aware of are those of practical meaning. As stated by thesis 5,

85 G.W.F. Hegel, *Hegel's Encyclopaedia of the Philosophical Sciences, Part One: The Shorter Logic*, Oxford: Oxford University Press, 1975, § 155–158.

one should conceive of 'sensuousness as *practical*, human-sensuous activity.' In other words, the primacy of the practical elaborated in the first thesis is grounded in a pragmatism conception of consciousness as always linked with our practical interactions with the environment, and in a pragmatist conception of objectivity, identifying objects as being primarily objects of practical activity and only secondarily as objects of theoretical consideration. The implications of these pragmatist insights concern the epistemological dimension of the primacy of the practical, which I will consider in the next section of this part.

The fact that thesis 1 is to be interpreted in phenomenological rather than ontological terms means that Marx's intention was not to elaborate a metaphysical position or a general ontology. But when thesis 8 claims that 'all social life is *essentially* practical', Marx clearly addresses social ontological issues. Indeed, it can be argued that all social ontology, as 'special ontology' or 'regional ontology', rely upon general assumptions belonging to general ontology. We have already noted that the most general ontological assumption of Marxian social theory probably consists of considering reciprocal action as a generic trait of reality. But it remains true that it is likely that Marx's intention was not to elaborate a theory of the generic traits of reality as such, but rather to make explicit the generic traits of *social* reality. And it is only in this respect that one can speak of the ontological dimension of the primacy of the practical. What specifies the social reality and contrasts it with other types of reality is that it is essentially linked with social practices such as labour and political action.[86]

The fact that 'social life is essentially practical' has to be understood in three different senses. Firstly, social reality is a natural reality transformed by specific transformative practices among which work plays a central role. In this first sense, social reality is essentially practical because it is produced by practices, mainly by working activities. Secondly, social reality is a set of practices. Each society is defined by a specific division of labour that organizes the activities of its members in order to satisfy the social needs of the various social groups set up by this division of labour. Shaped by this division of labour, social life consists in various types of 'intercourse (*Verkehr*) of individuals with one another.'[87] In this second sense, social reality is essentially practical not because it is caused by practices but rather because it consists of practices.

86 For a reading of Marx as a social ontologist, See C.C. Gould, *Marx's Social Ontology. Individuality and Community in Marx's Theory of Social Reality*, Cambridge, MA: MIT Press, 1975.

87 CW 5, 32.

Thirdly, some practices can be oriented toward social transformation, and they can succeed in transforming social reality. These transformations can be radical since 'revolutionary practice' can result in deep transformations of the social division of labour. In this third sense, social reality is essentially practical because it is specified by its capacity to be transformed in its very structures by practices.

Hence a first specificity of Marx's social ontological position: he thinks of the practical essence of social reality with reference to two distinct concepts of practice: practice as work and practice as revolutionary action. In the *Manuscripts of 1844* and in the first pages of *The German Ideology*, it is mainly work, labour, and production that come to the fore. Social life is depicted as being produced by work and organized by division of labour, and this account of the social is associated with a definition of men as *homo faber* or as 'tool making animals'.[88] As in the words of *The German Ideology*:

> Men can be distinguished from animals by consciousness, by religion or anything else you like. They themselves begin to distinguish themselves from animals as soon as they begin to produce their means of subsistence, a step which is conditioned by their physical organisation. By producing their means of subsistence men are indirectly producing their actual material life.[89]

In the *Thesis on Feuerbach*, there is no explicit reference to work or labour, and practice seems to be thought of mainly in terms of 'revolutionary practice'. Marx's point is that social practice in general is not only conditioned by subjective conditions, such as needs and social interests, and by objective conditions or 'circumstances' that make some actions necessary, either possible or impossible. Social action also has the potential of internal and external transformations, as is proved by the fact that revolutionary action has been possible in history. To put it as in thesis 3: 'The coincidence of the changing of circumstances and of human activity or self-change can be conceived and rationally understood only as *revolutionary practice*'.

There is no reason to consider that these two conceptions of practice, as work and revolutionary action, are mutually incompatible and imply conflicting accounts of the social. It is simply a fact that our ordinary practices consist

88 *Capital I*, 286: 'The use and construction of instruments of labour, although present in germ among certain species of animals, is characteristic of the specifically human labour process, and Franklin therefore defines man as "a tool-making animal".'

89 CW 5, 31.

mainly in working activities and of intercourses conditioned by our position in the social division of labour. If practice has to be thought of in its worldliness, it has to then be conceived of primarily as work. But it is also a fact that revolutionary actions are possible. This is the case because social reality is a type of reality that is produced by practices and that consists of practices, so that it can also be transformed by practices. Indeed, the transformations of the division of labour could be caused by economic dynamics that are usually not driven by revolutionary practices and these dynamics will also produce deep transformations in the superstructure and in ideology, that is in the rest of the social life. We will see in *Capital* that Marx precisely wants to spell out a set of 'laws' of social evolution that produce deep effects on social life without the intervention of practices consciously oriented toward social transformation. But it is also a fact that deep transformations of social life can also be produced by practices working toward such transformations. It is not only the dynamics that structure the division of labour that have the power to transform the social, revolutionary action can too.

The second specificity of Marx's social ontology is that it highlights the fact that the practicality of social life can be experienced by men and women in two opposite modes. Social reality, as a product of practices, can be experienced by individuals as the objectification of their own practices, as a reality that 'mirrors' their own capacities and help them satisfy their needs and fulfill their desire.[90] But it can also be experienced as an alien reality, a reality over which they have no control and that consists of a set of constraints that make it impossible to satisfy one's needs and to fulfil one's desires. The notion of 'alienated labour', elaborated in the first notebooks of the *Manuscripts of 1844* is precisely intended to describe the process through which the social reality produced by work becomes independent of the control of the working men and transforms itself into a social power oppressing the working men and mutilating their lives. In this context, the concept of 'alienation' denotes a twofold process: firstly, the process through which the product of one's activity becomes independent and transforms itself into an oppressive power; secondly, the process in which one sees his capacities reduced by his own activity instead of developing his capacities through his activities – a process

90 In 1844, Marx has precisely defined communism as a society in which individuals could mirror their 'species being' or human essence in their product or the products of others: 'In the individual expression of my life I would have directly created your expression of your life, and therefore in my individual activity I would have directly *confirmed* and *realised* my true nature, my *human* nature, my *communal being* (*Gemeinwesen*). Our products would be so many mirrors in which we saw reflected our essential nature' (CW 3, 228).

that can lead to an incapacity to recognize oneself in one's own actions and even in one's life and social environment. These two dimensions of the alienating process are put to the fore in the following quote:

> We have considered the act of alienating practical human activity, labour, in two of its aspects. (1) The relation of the worker to the *product of labour* as an alien object exercising power over him. This relation is as the same time the relation to the sensuous external world, to the objects of nature, as an alien world inimically opposed to him. (2) The relation of labour to the *act of production* within the *labour* process. This relation is the relations of the worker to his own activity as an alien activity not belonging to him; it is activity as suffering (...), his personal life – for what is life but activity – as an activity that is turned against him, independent of him and not belonging to him.[91]

It can be said that the objective side of this process entails some kind of 'world alienation', and the subjective side of this process entails some kind of 'self-alienation'. H. Arendt has charged Marx for having conceived of alienation only as subjective alienation (deprivation of one's own working activity) and not as world alienation.[92] But these two sides are intertwined in Marx's theory of alienated labour, and as such, this theory has many contemporary echoes. From a socio-psychological point of view, it is probably the case that the feeling of having become a stranger to myself (self-alienation) always goes with a feeling of living in a world that has become alien to myself, the world in which I have lost myself.[93] From a socio-theoretical point of view, it is also probably the case that when men have lost all control on the becoming of their societies, they also have probably lost control on their individual life and on the capacity of avoiding experiences of self-alienation.[94]

From a social ontological point of view the concept of alienation is also insightful. It raises an interesting paradox: socialized individuals could feel as strangers in the society that their actions contribute to produce and reproduce. It means that social life could become essentially contradictory: it is a reality produced and reproduced by social action, as well as a reality apparently independent of social action and undermining the capacities usually associated with social action. Or to put it in the terms of contemporary social ontology:

---

91 CW 3, 275.

92 H. Arendt, *The Human Condition*, Chicago: The University of Chicago Press, 1998, 248–256.

93 R. Jaeggi, *Alienation*, New York: Columbia University Press, 2014.

94 S. Haber, *Penser le néocapitalisme. Vie, capital et aliénation*, Paris : Prairies ordinaires, 2013.

society is objectified action and reality structured by the meanings one gives to his own actions, but it is also the reified reality of meaningless actions and institutions. On the one hand, society is objectified action since institutions are produced by practices, and since it is structured by the meaning one gives to his own actions for actions always have a meaning for their authors: even alienated labour has the meaning of the social activity necessary to earn one's living. But on the other hand, society is also a set of institutions and products (goods and services) over which the vast majority of the population has lost control – as if they were just as independent of human practices as natural beings, a "reified second nature", to use the terms of Frankfurt critical theory, which can be experienced as a set of meaningless constraints.[95] With the notion of alienation, a new implication of the contention that social life is essentially practical comes to the fore. This contention has not only a descriptive but also a normative meaning which depends precisely on the fact that the practicality of social life can be alienated or not. The very notion of alienation presupposes a conception of social reality as produced by human activity, but with his notion of 'alienated labour', Marx wants to highlight fact that until now, in the history of human beings, social life has always been structured by some kind of contradiction between human practices and their product. In other words, social life has never been truly practical or essentially practical in the sense of conforming to its essence. In this respect, the very notion of alienation is a means of justifying revolutionary social transformations from a social ontological point of view. It calls for a transformation of the alienated into non-alienated social life.

This last remark leads us to the third specificity of Marx's social ontology that has probably become one of the trademarks of all critical theories: Marx thinks of the social in the perspective of its transformation, and more precisely, in the perspective of its revolutionary transformation.[96] The logic of the materialist conception of practice implies that this possibility has to be conceived of in a twofold perspective, the first of which is that of a theory of the revolutionary potential of social practice. The second perspective is that of a social theory of

95 T.W. Adorno has retained from Marx that a social theory of capitalism should combine this too opposite points of views on the social: social as objectified meanings, and social as reified second nature. He has criticized Weber for adopting only the first of these points of views, and Durkheim only the second. See for instance his article "Gesellschaft", *Gesammelte Schriften*, volume 8, Frankfurt: Suhrkamp, 2003, 9–19.

96 On the implications of such a point of view for contemporary social ontological discussions, see E. Renault, "Critical theory and processual social ontology", *Journal of Social Ontology*, Volume 2, Issue 1, 2016, 17–32.

the circumstances of revolutionary practice. I will describe more precisely the principles of Marx's social theory in the next part. For the time being, it suffices to mention that Marx thinks of societies as a totality of mediations, or reciprocal actions, as well as a totality of contradictions. The structural contradictions of a society, as well as the structural dynamics and the social conflicts emerging from these contradictions, are precisely what produce the circumstances compatible with revolutionary practice. And this is also probably a trademark of all critical theories: conceiving of societies not only as harmonious totalities (a collective mind, a set of collective representations, a network of solidarity, etc.), but also as a set of social antagonisms and social conflicts.[97]

The materialist account of revolutionary practice also requires a theory of the subjective conditioning of practice in general and revolutionary practice in particular. Actions are driven mainly by needs and interests. Ideas and ideologies could also play a role, but they are only secondary factors. In *A Contribution to the Critique of Hegel's Philosophy of Law. Introduction*, one reads: 'the needs of the nations are in themselves the ultimate reason for their satisfaction.'[98] In chapter VI of *The Holy Family*, Marx writes that '[t]he idea always disgraced itself insofar as it differed from the "interest".'[99] And in chapter IV of the same book, it is both with reference to needs and social interest that Marx points out that:

> It is not a question of what this or that proletarian, or even the whole proletariat, at the moment regards as its aim. It is a question of what the proletariat is, and what, in accordance with this being, it will historically be compelled to do. Its aim and historical action are visibly and irrevocably foreshadowed in its own life situation as well as in the whole organization of bourgeois society today.[100]

This theory of the primary role of needs and interests has a naturalist as well as sociological moment since needs have a natural as well as social dimension. In the *Manuscripts of 1844*, Marx highlights that human beings, like any other natural being, are *beings in need*.[101] But their needs also have a social dimension. The development of the social division of labour and the specialisation

97 See for instance Adorno, "Anmerkungen zum sozialen Konflikt heute", GS 8, 177–195.
98 CW 3, 178.
99 CW 4, 81.
100 CW 4, 37.
101 CW 3, 304.

of production creates new needs corresponding to new products or services. Moreover, social evolutions can produce a degradation of human needs as well as a sophistication of these needs. And indeed, social position also plays a role: the social position of a proletarian or capitalist impacts their needs. In *Capital*, Marx mentions again the questions of the sociality of needs in the discussion of the definition of the value of labour-power as the quantity of labour necessary to its reproduction: he explains that the needs to fulfil in order to reproduce labour-power depend on social and historical conditions.[102]

Practice is driven not only by natural and social needs, but also by social interests. This fact becomes obvious in the case of revolutionary practices. The ruling classes are interested in the preservation of the *status quo*, whereas the oppressed classes are interested in the structural transformation of the society in which they are oppressed. According to Marx, the social interests of the proletarians cannot be satisfied but by revolutionary practices intending to substitute a communist society for a capitalist society. Hence, in the case of the revolutionary struggles of the proletariat, the social interest appears as the most decisive factor. But needs also play their role in the constitution of the proletariat as a revolutionary force, for social interest and needs are hardly separable in this case. In fact, it is precisely because the situation of the working class makes it impossible to fulfill basics needs related to food, housing, and health that workers have a social interest in social transformation. To put it as *Wages, Price and profit*:

> The very development of modern industry must progressively turn the scale in favour of the capitalist against the working man, and consequently the general tendency of capitalistic production is not to raise, but to sink the average standard of wages, or to push the *value of labour* more or less to its *minimum limit*. Such being the tendency of things in this system, is this saying that the working class ought to renounce their

102 *Capital I*, 275: 'If the owner of labour-power works today, tomorrow he must again be able to repeat the same process in the same conditions as regards health and strength. His means of subsistence must therefore be sufficient to maintain him in his normal state as a working individual. His natural needs, such as food, clothing, fuel, and housing vary according to the climatic and other physical peculiarities of his country. On the other hand, the number and extent of his so-called necessary requirements, as also the modes of satisfying them, are themselves products of history, and depend therefore to a great extent on the level of civilization attained by a country; in particular they depend on the conditions in which, and consequently on the habits and expectations with which, the class of free workers has been formed. In contrast, therefore, with the case of other commodities, the determination of the value of labour-power contains a historical and moral element.'

> resistance against the encroachments of capital, and abandon their attempts at making the best of the occasional chances for their temporary improvement? If they did, they would be degraded to one level mass of broken wretches past salvation.[103]

The coincidence of the objective conditions for revolutionary action (development of structural contradictions) with its subjective conditions (situation of unsatisfied basic needs and interest) defines the 'real possibility' of communism; 'real possibility' being understood here in its Hegelian sense in contrast with the abstract of formal possibility: not only a logical possibility but also a possibility with regard to the conditions of its actualisation.[104] According to Marx, communism isn't only an abstract or formal possibility, it is a real possibility defined by the set of subjective and objective conditions of its own actualisation, and a possibility already engaged in the process of its own actualisation. This discloses one of the meanings of the famous definition of communism provided by *The German Ideology*: 'Communism is for us not a *state of affairs* which is to be established, an *ideal* to which reality [will] have to adjust itself. We call communism the *actual* movement which abolishes the present state of things. The conditions of this movement result from the now existing premises.'[105] Thinking of emancipation in terms of 'real possibilities', rather than simply referring to an abstract 'ought', criticizing the present state of things not only from a normative point of view but also from a cognitive point of view, that is, with a reference to knowledge of the emancipatory potentialities located in the present state of affairs, this also is constitutive of critical theory.[106] In summation: the transformative potential of practice depends on a set of subjective and objective conditions of social transformation. One implication of this general contention is that if practice has a transformative potential, it is not always transformative. It is simply a fact that alienated societies are largely out of the control of individual and collective action, so that it is always a real challenge to produce deep social transformations by collective action. It is also a fact that the subjective and objective conditions for revolutionary action are not always met. Moreover, even for those who are

103 CW 20, 148.

104 G.W.F. Hegel, *Hegel's Encyclopaedia of the Philosophical Sciences, Part One: The Shorter Logic*, § 147.

105 CW 5, 49.

106 See for instance H. Marcuse, *Reason and Revolution*, p. 149–154; E. Bloch, *The Principle of Hope*, vol. 1, ch. 17–18.

in need of revolutionary action and who are confronted a situation when the structural contradictions have matured, many other factors could create obstacles to revolutionary practice: social factors, for example, like the isolation of the proletarians subjected to competition for jobs; or social factors like the forms of structural domination that oblige the proletarians themselves to participate in the reproduction of the capitalist order if they want to earn their living; or like technical and political power-dispositions that compel them to obey the boss in the factory and the government out of the factory. Cognitive factors also play a role, for instance, ideological factors that present capitalism as the only rational organisation of the economic basis of society or as being grounded in a set of human rights. These cognitive factors plainly show that practice is not only driven by needs and interests but also by the representations of the contemporary world. It implies that revolutionary practice has to be accompanied not only by a practical knowledge of the means at disposal in order to achieve structural transformations, but also by a theoretical criticism of the ideological factors that tend to depict the present state of affair as necessary and plainly legitimate. In this respect, revolutionary practice depends of some kind of unity between theory and practice.

Epistemological Primacy of the Practical

The thesis of the unity of theory and practice has a descriptive as well as a normative side. On the descriptive side, Marx contends that theory always depends on practice in its form, in its content, and in its validity. This is true of all theoretical activity, be it pure or applied, be it conceived as independent of practice or not. But the thesis of theory/practice unity is not intended to only describe a general feature of theoretical activity. It is also intended, on the normative side, to define the ways in which theoretical activities should become aware of their practice dependency and in which theoretical activities should connect themselves to a certain type of practice, namely revolutionary practice. In what follows, I will consider the descriptive meaning of theory/practice unity before considering its normative dimensions and the nature of the link between theory and revolutionary practice.

Marx rejects the traditional assumption of theory as an activity detached from any practical activity and as having and immanent end, namely the truth of the theory. In other words, he does not believe that theory is a disinterested or impartial search for the truth. His point is that all theory is dependent on practical interests and rooted in social interests. Like Hegel, Marx knows that everybody belongs to his own time, and that it is impossible, from a practical point of view as well from a theoretical point of view, to 'leap out of his time'.[107] Marx's conception of theory/practice unity is part of the presentist orientation of his philosophy, and this presentism is inherited from Hegel, as already mentioned in part 1. The difference with Hegel is that Marx does not believe that contemporary societies are on the verge of becoming rational totalities or that the 'spirit of the time' (*Zeitgeist*) is a unified spirit. On the contrary, contemporary societies are contradictory totalities, and the 'spirit of the time' is fractured by the clash of social interests. In *The German Ideology*, the notion of ideology is precisely intended to shed light on the dependence of ideas, in general on the conflicting social interests of the ruling classes and the dominated classes. The ruling ideas in any epoch are always the ideas of the ruling class:

> The ideas of the ruling class are in every epoch the ruling ideas, i.e., the class which is the ruling *material* force of society, is at the same time its ruling *intellectual* force. The class which has the means of material production at its disposal, consequently also has control the means of mental production, so that the ideas of those who lack the means of mental production are on the whole subject to it. The ruling ideas are nothing more than the ideal expression of the dominant material relations, the dominant material relations grasped as ideas.[108]

The link between the ruling ideas of an epoch and the ruling classes is presented here as an expressive link: the ruling classes control the production of ideas (via the intellectual professions) as well as the reproduction of ideas (via the educational systems) and these ideas express their social interests. This expression is twofold. Firstly, it concerns the worldview that is associated to their position in society. In other words, the notion of ideology entails what could be termed, in the words of contemporary feminist critical theory, a standpoint epistemology.[109] All theoretical activity is dependent on a particular social standpoint that generates fundamental assumptions about the nature of reality and the subject-matters deserving consideration. All situated knowledge is limited by a specific horizon that makes it a partial knowledge. It is in this sense, for instance, that *Capital* speaks of the 'bounds of the bourgeois horizon'[110] as an obstacle to the scientific investigation of the capitalist

107 G.W.F. Hegel, *The Philosophy of Right*, Kitchener: Batoche, 2001, 19.

108 CW 5, 59.

109 See for instance D. Haraway, "Situated Knowledge: The Science Question in Feminism and the Privilege of Partial Perspective", *Feminist Studies*, Volume 14, Issue 3, 1988, 575–599.

110 *Capital I*, p. 96.

economy, and he wants to overcome this horizon by taking another social standpoint, that of the proletariat. The notion of ideology adds that the ruling class has not only a specific horizon, but it also tries to present the worldview defined by this horizon as the only legitimate one.[111]

Secondly, ideologies also express a social interest in so far as they fulfill a function that is defined by the social interests of the ruling classes. The ruling classes are interested in justifying their own social position and the entire social organisation from which they benefit. In Marx, the concept of ideology precisely denotes the justificatory function of the ruling ideas. It denotes a particular form of justification, in which the domination of the rest of society by the ruling classes is presented as something that benefits all. Ideology is therefore synonymous with some kind of inversion of the relationship between the particular and the general: the particular interests of the ruling class are depicted as being in the interest of all.

> Each new class which puts itself in the place of one ruling before it is compelled, merely in order to carry through its aim, to present its interest as the common interest of all the members of society, that is, expressed in ideal form: it has to give its ideas the form of universality, and represent them as the only rational, universally valid ones.[112]

It is worth noting that the fact that in each epoch, the ruling ideas are the ideas of the ruling class does not mean that all social classes are equally convinced of the ideological justification of the particular interests of the ruling class. Ideology does not mean consensus, and in its intellectual dimension also, social life is structured by structural contradictions and conflicts. Indeed, the function of ideology is to provide justifications that are able to undermine the criticisms of domination that emerge from the dominated classes. But it does not imply that the ideological justifications succeed in convincing the members of the dominated classes that the domination they are suffering from is legitimate. Marx's standpoint epistemology implies to the contrary that only the members of the ruling classes could be completely convinced by ideological justifications. It is in this sense that Marx writes in the *Communist Manifesto* that the proletariat has no ideological illusions because they are not compatible with

---

111 Hence a possible comparison with Bourdieu's sociology of social conflicts has consisting, in its cognitive side, in struggles between groups over the legitimacy of their own worldviews. For a discussion of Bourdieu from the point of view of the Marxian concept of ideology, see T. Eagleton, *Ideology. An Introduction*, London: Verso, 1991, ch. 5.

112 CW 5, 60.

its own living conditions: 'Law, morality, religion, are to him so many bourgeois prejudices, behind which lurk in ambush just as many bourgeois interests.'[113] The same idea was expressed in *The German Ideology*, with regard to the religious ideologies that the Young Hegelian wanted to destroy by theoretical means:

> The real, practical dissolution of these [religious] phrases, the removal of these notions from the consciousness of men, will, as we have already said, be effected by altered circumstance, not by theoretical deductions. For the mass of men, i.e., the proletariat, these theoretical notions do not exist and hence do not require to be dissolved, and if this mass ever had any theoretical notions, e.g., religion, these have now long been dissolved by circumstances.[114]

In other words, Marx' standpoint epistemology implies that the ruling ideas cannot really fulfill their ideological function in the dominated classes. These classes are defined by a social interest oriented toward social transformation, and such an interest generates a critical perspective on the ideological justifications of the present social order. It results that the clash of social interests affects the form of the theoretical activity. The social interests of the ruling classes tend to generate theories oriented toward the justification of the existing social order. The social interests of the dominated classes tend to generate theories that criticise the existing social order as well as its ideological justification. As we will see, *Capital* is working toward these two goals, and it is in this sense that Marx can claim that his critique of political economy is expressing the social interest of the proletariat and shares its standpoint:

> In so far as such a critique represents a class, it can only represent the class whose historical task is to overthrow of the capitalist mode of production and the final abolition of all classes – the proletariat.[115]

Hence, theory is conditioned not only by practice in its content, in the basic assumptions and horizon of each theoretical production, but also in its form – some social standpoints give rise to justificatory theories while others to critical theories. Finally, theory is also dependent on practice for its validity, that is,

113 CW 6, 481.
114 CW 5, 56.
115 *Capital I*, 98.

for its truth. Now it is precisely concerning this latter dependency that theory/practice unity implies an epistemological primacy of the practical.

I have already quoted the third of the *Theses on Feuerbach* and its pragmatist account of truth: 'Man must prove the truth – i.e. the reality and power, the this-worldliness of his thinking in practice.' The best way to read this thesis is to remember that theory is always oriented by practical interests, and therefore, always has a practical function, namely, theory has to help in working toward the satisfaction of some practical interests. Now the notion that describes the type of validity that is proper to theoretical activity is truth. Therefore, it can be said that truth depends on the ability of theory to fulfill its practical function. According to such a reading, the third thesis on Feuerbach does not equate truth with practical efficiency or with experimental confirmation, but with the unity of theory with its practical function, that is, with the capacity of theory to help satisfy some practical interests that drive social practices.

Just as all theoretical activity is oriented either toward justification of the existing social order or toward its critique, so too the truth of a particular theoretical activity is always conditioned by its relations with the practices oriented by the particular social interests that are expressed in this theoretical activity, for this theory cannot fulfill its functions if it does not produce effects on these practices. But in Marx, the thesis of theory/practice unity is not only intended to spell out the general features that make theoretical activity dependent on practice for its truth. It is also intended to promote a transformation of the traditional mode of theoretical activity. Traditionally, it is considered that theory must only orient itself toward knowing truth and the essence of justice and freedom, or conversely, toward criticism of the false, the unjust, and unfree. According to Marx, it must also reflect on its form, on its content, and its objectives. More precisely, Marx's normative concept of theory entails a threefold self-reflection.

Firstly, it entails a reflection of theory on its own relations with the ruling ideas of the epoch and on the social interests it expresses. Marx's normative concept of theory entails a second type of self-reflection: a reflection on the discrepancies of some of its traditional assumptions with the present situation. The existing world is a world of structural injustice and domination, and these injustices and dominations are depicted by the ruling ideas as justice and freedom, so that the existing world is not only structurally unjust and unfree, but also essentially untrue.[116] Therefore, the theoretical activity must not

116 In the tradition of critical theory, Adorno is the one who has analyzed most deeply the consequences of the fact that contemporary society is "untrue" for the philosophical project. Note that in Adorno, the existing social order is not only "untrue" because it is

only orient itself toward the interpretation of the rationality or irrationality of the existing world, but toward its practical transformation. To put is as in thesis 11: 'The philosophers have only *interpreted* the world, in various ways; the point would be to *change* it.' In order to contribute to the transformation of the existing world, theory must criticize it (to depict it as untrue, as unjust, and as unfree), but also criticize its justification and think of this existing world in the perspective of its own transformation. Critical theory then means social critique, critique of ideology, and knowledge of the contradictions and the real possibilities of emancipation that are specific to the present situation. To contribute to social transformation via theoretical means also implies rejecting the traditional conception of theory as the impartial interpretation of the rationality or irrationality of the world. The real possibility of an emancipatory transformation of the existing social order depends on an emancipatory interest, and philosophy must therefore take the side of the social group driven by such an interest. In the words of a letter of Marx to Ruge: 'nothing prevents us from making (...) *real* struggles the starting point of our criticism, and from identifying our criticism with them.'[117]

This leads us to the third type of self-reflection that is required if theory really wants to contribute to transforming the existing world. In fact, theory cannot change the world by itself; only practice has such a transformative power. To put it as in *Critique of Hegel's Philosophy of Law. Introduction*: 'The weapon of criticism cannot, of course, replace criticism by weapons, material force must be overthrown by material force; but theory also becomes a material force as soon it has gripped the masses.'[118] Therefore, critical theory must reflect on the ways in which it could become useful to emancipatory practices and hence participate in social transformation. It should become aware that it can become useful to transformative practices in providing them the knowledge of the 'real possibilities' of emancipation they need, and in criticising the ideological obstacles they are confronted with. Critical theory has a deficit of transformative power in itself, as theory, since social life is essentially practical and social transformation is a matter of practice more than of theory. But conversely, revolutionary practices are confronted with cognitive problems

irrational or not adequate with what one should expect from a society. It is untrue also because it appears, ideologically, as rational and adequate to what one should expect from a society. Essentially untrue, society presents itself as true, dissimulating that its essence is a non-essential reality. See T.W. Adorno, *Negative Dialectics*, New York: Routledge, 2004, 166–167.

117 CW 3, 144.

118 CW 3, 182.

and obstacles whose solution is of a theoretical nature. In this respect, critical theory and transformative practices are in need of each other.

This reciprocal need implies that it is misleading to search for an immediate unity of theory and practice. Each of them is mediated by the other, and neither of them should try to relegate the other to a secondary position.[119] Marx rejects the two opposite ways of thinking of the unity of theory and practice as immediate unity, the first of which attributes a primacy to the theoretical, and the second a primacy of the practical. According to a first model, theory comes first, and practice is relegated to a secondary position, as mere application of theory. According to Auguste Comte's famous dictum, for instance, 'From science comes prevision, from prevision comes action' (*theory d'où prévision, prévision d'où action*). Then practice is reduced to mere application of theory and is deprived of all immanent dynamics. Conversely, theory is autonomous in its development. But as noted before, according to Marx, practices are driven primarily by needs and interests, not by ideas. Moreover, far from being autonomous, theory is dependent on practice for its truth and its transformative power.

Therefore, it could seem that Marx would be led to the opposite position that reduces theory to a mere tool for action, as if critical theory was totally at the service of a practice driven by an emancipatory interest. Indeed, in some passages, Marx seems to endorse this conception of the unity of theory and practice, for instance in the *Critique of Hegel's Philosophy of Law. Introduction* when he suggests that all theoretical means are legitimate as soon as they are practically efficient: 'Criticism (…) is criticism in *hand to hand combat*, and in such a fight, the point is not whether the opponent is a noble, equal, *interesting* opponent, the point is to strike him.'[120] Here, the norms of theoretical activity are apparently reduced to that of practical efficiency in social struggles ('*the hand to hand combat*' with the social groups who endeavour to preserve the existing order). But a careful reading of the *Critique of Hegel's Philosophy of Law. Introduction* reveals that Marx's conception of theory/practice unity is much more mediated. It is simply a fact that in this text, Marx was not already associating the unity of theory and practice with the primacy of the practical. On the contrary, at that time, Marx remained enough of a Hegelian to attribute to philosophical theory some kind of primacy over the practical struggles of

119 See T.W. Adorno, "Marginalia to Theory and Praxis", *Critical Models*, New York: Columbia University Press, 1998, 259–278.

120 CW 3, 178.

the proletariat.[121] It is not before the *Theses on Feuerbach* that he elaborated his conception of the ontological and epistemological primacy of the practical.

Now, in the *Theses on Feuerbach* and in the mature Marx, the epistemological primacy of the practical is associated with a conception of a mediated unity of theory and practice. Theory is not reduced to a practical instrument subordinated to practical norms. On the contrary, it is because it has its own norms, which make it relatively autonomous, that theoretical activity could be useful to practice. Knowledge of the social order to be transformed, critique of ideological justification of this social order, and self-reflection are subjected to specific norms that are irreducible to practical efficiency. In Marx, the knowledge of the social order to be transformed, namely the theory of capitalism elaborated in *Capital*, intends to be knowledge in the emphatic sense of the term, namely, scientific knowledge. *Capital* claims to be scientific in its methods and objectives and to be the only scientific contemporary development of the scientific tradition in political economy: classical political economy. It is precisely because it is elaborated in conformity with scientific norms that are not norms of practical efficiency, that *Capital* provides a knowledge that could be useful to revolutionary practices.

Critique of ideology also has its own relative autonomy. To fulfill its function, ideological discourses have to present themselves as rational, whatever the form they take. Ideological discourses could present themselves as grounded in the highest moral or religious principles, for instance when the 'right to private property' is presented as a 'human right' by the philosophies of natural rights and by the 'declaration of the rights of the man and the citizen'. But they could also present themselves as grounded on scientific truth, for instance when classical political economy depicts the laws of capitalist production as natural laws. Therefore, in order to criticize ideology as such, it is enough neither to unveil the social interests expressed and dissimulated in the ruling ideas nor to denounce their practical effects. One must show that their validity claim is not legitimate since it goes with an erroneous conception of society.[122] For instance, the legitimation of the capitalist order, as based on the legal principles of individual freedom and equality, dissimulates the fact that

121 See for instance, CW 3, 187: 'As philosophy finds its *material* weapons in the proletariat, so the proletariat finds its *spiritual* weapons in philosophy. And once the lightning of thought has squarely struck this ingenious soil of the people the emancipation of the *Germans* into *human beings* will take place'.

122 T.W. Adorno claims in this sense that critique of ideology should not be confused with relativist sociology of knowledge, and shouldn't renounce to the reference to truth: see *Negative Dialectics*, 197–198.

there is a structural inequality between owners and non-owners of the means of production, and that this inequality compels the proletarians to consent to wage-work and the correlated domination in the workplaces – workplaces that are not regulated by the legal principles of individual freedom and equality. But to unmask this untruth of the legal principles,[123] ideology critique has to ground itself in knowledge concerning the reasons why the proletarian have to consent to wage-work and in the nature of wage-work. Similarly, in order to criticize the justification of capitalism as the actualization of the rational laws of production, one has to show that the so-called natural laws of capitalist production are historical rather than natural, since they describe mechanisms that are conditioned by structural inequalities specific to the capitalist societies. Then, with ideology critique, we see that if critical theory can be useful to transformative practices, undermining the ideological obstacle they meet, it is only because theory addresses the issue of the truth of ideological justification in terms that do not equate truth with practical efficiency.

This is all the more evident in the third dimension of critical theory, the one that concerns self-reflection. The moment of the self-reflection of the theory is the moment it gains autonomy: in self-reflection, theory relates to itself. But, as already noted, in the type of self-reflection that specifies critical theory, self-reflection is also a reflection on something that is not theoretical in nature: on the one hand, the social interests that express themselves in ideas and theories, on the other hand, the transformative practices with which critical theory should try to unite. In this respect, self-reflection is paradoxically autonomous as well as heteronomous. At first glance, the type of self-reflection Marx has in view produces it effects only on theoretical discourses, helping them to change their objectives and methods in order to become useful for transformative practices. Then it is only indirectly useful for these practices. But theoretical activity can also try to reflect social interests, as well as the normative and cognitive assumptions of the transformative practices. In this respect, it can become the theoretical self-reflection of these practices. This kind of self-reflection also characterizes Marx's conception of critical theory. By self-reflection of the cognitive assumptions of the transformative practices, I mean a critical examination of the conceptions of the nature of contemporary societies that are presupposed by the worker movement. For instance, is it to assume that 'Labour is the source of all wealth and all culture', as in the *Gotha's Program*[124]? Marx answers no. Wrong assumptions of this type could lead to political dead ends. Therefore, it can be considered that it is the very

123 I will discuss the nature of this untruth in the next part.

124 CW 24, 81–82.

dynamics of revolutionary practices in their efforts to overcome the tactic, strategic, and programmatic problems they are confronted with that calls for a critical examination of these assumptions. That is the reason why Marx has always thought of his critique of political economy as participating in some kind of theoretical self-reflection of revolutionary practices.

The same is true for the theoretical reflection on the interests of the working class, as it is elaborated in *The German Ideology* and the *Communist Manifesto*. In these texts, Marx tries to show that the proletariat is not a dominated class as others. The gist of his argument is that the capitalist society is structured by a simplification of class antagonism. In capitalism, at least tendentially, there is only one ruling class, the bourgeoisie, and one dominated class, the proletariat. In this particular historical situation, the proletariat cannot emancipate itself by becoming a new ruling class, as the dominated classes of the past did, but only by overcoming class domination itself. Marx's theory of history as the history of class struggles enables him to reflect on the specific nature of the social interests of the proletariat, and to criticise the forms of socialism and communism that are based either on misconceptions of these interests or misconceptions of the historical task of the worker movement. Hence the criticism, in the last part of the *Manifesto*, of the Feudal Socialists, the Petty-Bourgeois Socialists, the German or 'True' Socialists, the Conservative or Bourgeois Socialism, and the Critical-Utopian Socialism and Communism. The worker movement is confronted with a conflict between various socialist and communist orientations in which it is obliged to take sides, and there is no other way to take sides in such debates but by theoretical means. Here again, Marx's materialist conception of history can be conceived of as the self-reflection of revolutionary practice. As a matter of fact, Marx conceived the materialist conception of history he was delineating in the *Manifesto* as a theoretical tool intended to participate in the self-reflection of the worker movement on its specific interests and on the best ways to achieve a social transformation conforming to its interests.

Last but not least, this self-reflection entails a normative moment. Among the internal debates of the worker movement, the norms that should drive revolutionary practices were also at issue. Should they be religious norms enunciating the dignity of human beings, or the demand for freedom and equality that has been proclaimed by the "Declaration of the human rights", or a definition of social justice? Marx intervenes in these debates with two distinct arguments, the first of which relates to ideology criticism. Religious norms, just as the "Declaration of human rights", or the definition of justice as rewards proportional to merits are ideological, and therefore, they should not be taken as reference points by the revolutionaries. Hence the criticism of religious and humanist socialisms, and hence also the contention of the *Critique of the Gotha Program*: '*equal right* is still in principle – *bourgeois right*.'[125] The second argument concerns theory of action rather than ideology critique: revolutionary practice should not be conceived of as the mere application of normative principles but rather as a practice driven by needs and social interests. This does not mean that these practice are deprived of all normative content and that this normative content cannot be articulated in normative terms.[126] As a matter of fact, in the *Critique of the Gotha Program*, Marx is not afraid of describing which normative principles should orient the construction of the communist society. In a genuinely communist society, labour should become the prime need of men, and the goods and services should be distributed not in proportion of the contribution of individuals to the wealth of society, that is according to a bourgeois definition of justice, but in proportion of their needs:

> After the enslaving subordination of the individual to the division of labour, and thereby also the antithesis between mental and physical labour, has vanished; after labour has become not only a means of life but life's prime want; after the productive forces have also increased with the all-round development of the individual, and all the springs of common wealth flow more abundantly – only then can the narrow horizon of bourgeois right be crossed in its entirety and society inscribe on its banners: From each according to his ability, to each according to his needs![127]

In other words, Marx's point is that revolutionary practices should be driven by their immanent norms, neither by religious, legal, or moral principles, nor by utopian definitions of the ideal society. Revolutionary practices have to produce by themselves the normative principles that could help them achieve their goals, and it is in this respect that theoretical activity could be useful. There is no doubt that Marx thought of himself as participating in this kind of self-reflection of the worker movement when he was elaborating his critique of ideology and its subsequent critique of religious and moral socialisms and communisms, and also when he was highlighting that revolutionary practices find their ultimate justification in their own normative content and in the 'real

125 CW 24, 86.

126 Marxist scholarship has often raised the following problem: isn't it inconsistent to subject normative principles to ideology critique while elaborating a social critique that necessarily assumes normative presupposition. For a synthesis on these issues, see A. Wood, *Marx*, New York: Routledge, 2004, Part 3: "Marxism and Morality".

127 CW 24, 87.

possibilities' they are striving to actualise. This also discloses the meaning of his definition of communism, already quoted: 'Communism is for us not a *state of affairs* which is to be established, an *ideal* to which reality [will] have to adjust itself. We call communism the *actual* movement which abolishes the present state of things. The conditions of this movement result from the now existing premises.'[128]

I have just insisted on the fact that the moment that makes theoretical activity relatively autonomous, namely self-reflection, is also a moment where the primacy of the practical is at play. Since Marx conceived the forms of theoretical self-reflection he was elaborating a set of instruments for the self-reflection of revolutionary struggles. Such a conception of self-reflection has epistemological implications: it entails a critical conception of theory that is at odds with the traditional conception of theory. It also has political implications. Ultimately, revolutionary struggles must remain autonomous in the sense that theory should remain a moment, and only a moment, of their own self-reflection. To put it like the third thesis, the producers of theory should not behave like educators to whom the socialist and communist workers should obey in order to emancipate themselves. On the contrary, the producers of theory have to be educated by the revolutionary workers. They have to learn which theoretical means could be useful for the self-emancipation of the workers. From a political point of view, what is at stake in the Marxian conception of the unity of theory with practice is nothing else than a definition of emancipation as self-emancipation. In 1864, as the first premise of the Rules of the First International, Marx wrote: 'Considering, that the emancipation of the working classes must be conquered by the working classes themselves'. Self-emancipation is here presented as a political principle, if not as the main political principle. In the *Critique of the Gotha Program*, dated 1875, Marx recalls that in the 'introductory words of the Rules of the International (…) it is said: "The emancipation of the working class must be the act of the workers themselves".'[129] Later, in the 1888 preface to the *Communist Manifesto*, Engels says that 'our notion, from the very beginning, was that "the emancipation of the working class must be the act of the working class itself".'[130] Self-emancipation is depicted by Marx and Engels as one of the most important political principles, a principle that defines socialism from below and that articulates

128 CW 5, 49.

129 CW 24, 88.

130 See H. Draper, *Marx's Theory of Revolution*, New York: Monthly Review Press, 1978, Volume 2, Ch. 8: "The Principle of Class Self-Emancipation".

the anarchist moment of their political thought. They elaborated this principle with reference to the emancipatory struggles of the proletariat, but this principle has undoubted validity for many other dominated groups. As noted at the end of the first part, the feminist movements and the anti-racist movements have provided many illustrations of that. This definition of emancipation as self-emancipation, just as Marx's reflection on the epistemological implications of such a definition of emancipation, belongs to the Marxian deposit in contemporary critical theory.

Part 3: Critique of Political Economy

In the preceding part, I started to analyze the specificity of Marx's materialism. It consists of a materialist conception of history according to which social life is essentially practical and social practices are conditioned by ideological, legal, political, and economic constraints, the latter playing the most decisive role. Hence the famous description of societies as composed of three layers in the preface of *A contribution to the critique of political economy*:

> In the social production of their existence, men inevitably enter into definite relations, which are independent of their will, namely relations of production appropriate to a given stage in the development of *their material forces of production*. The totality of these relations of production constitutes the economic structure of society, the real foundation, on which arises a legal and political superstructure and to which correspond definite forms of social consciousness.[131]

According to such a conception of the organization of society, the economic basis of society is the structuring moment that shapes the legal, political and ideological moments of the social life. There is a 'reciprocal action'[132] between the structural, the superstructural, and ideological moments of social life,

---

131 CW 28, 263.

132 CW 5, 53: 'This conception of history thus relies on expounding the real process of production – starting form the material production of life itself – and comprehending the form of intercourse connected with and created by this mode of production, i.e., civil society in its various stages, as the basis of history; describing it in its action as the state and also explaining how the different theoretical products and forms of consciousness, religion, philosophy, morality, etc., etc., arise from it, and tracing the process of their

since for instance, a political revolution, which presupposes a series of ideological conflicts, is necessary to change the economic structure of society. But nevertheless, it is the economic moment that plays the prominent role in this reciprocal action. To take the same example, it is only when the economic contradictions of society have reached a high level of intensity, and when the conditions for a new mode of production have matured, that political and ideological conflicts of a revolutionary nature can take place:

> The mode of production of material life conditions the general process of social, political and intellectual life. It is not the consciousness of men that determines their existence, but their social existence that determines their consciousness. At a certain stage of development, the material productive forces of society come into conflict with the existing relations of production or – this merely expresses the same thing in legal terms – with the property relations within the framework of which they have operated hitherto. From forms of development of the productive forces these relations turn into their fetters. Then begins an era of social revolution. The changes in the economic foundation lead sooner or later to the transformation of the whole immense superstructure. (…). No social order is ever destroyed before all the productive forces for which it is sufficient have been developed, and new superior relations of production never replace older ones before the material conditions for their existence have matured within the framework of the old society.[133]

According to this materialist account of social organization and evolution, the whole development of history is to be explained by the dialectics between the development of the productive forces and the social relations of production. By productive forces, Marx means the productive capacity of work, division of labour, and technologies. Marx conceives of history as a constant development of these productive forces, and this has subjected him to harsh criticism. He has been accused of assuming that history is some kind of homogeneous development and quantitative progress, as if he believed, just as the philosophers of history, that all social evolutions were subordinated to one and the same goal, namely the development of the productive forces. There is no doubt that Marx's conception of history entails some kind of faith in technological progress and economic growth and that is should be criticized for that. But

---

formation from that basis; thus the whole thing can, of course, be depicted in its totality (and therefore, too, the reciprocal action of these various sides on one another).'

133 CW 28, 263.

it remains that he has correctly perceived the tendency in history to always increase the productive power of labour, as well as its paradoxical effect: instead of decreasing the degree of exploitation of nature and of human beings, this progress of the productive forces has always more destroyed nature[134] and has increased the exploitation of the labour-power force. There is some kind of "dialectics of enlightenment"[135] in Marx's conception of history as the development of productive forces: instead of making better our relations with nature and emancipating men, the progress of technological reason has produced more destruction of nature and has increased the social centrality of the exploitation of men by men.

According to Marx, the various epochs of historical development have to be defined, in materialist terms, with reference to the concept of "modes of production". Each mode of production is specified by a level of the development of the productive forces and corresponding social relations of production. By social relation of production, he means the type of property of the means of production and labour-power that opposes one or many exploited classes to one or many exploiting classes. For instance, in the Antique mode of production, the slave neither owns his own labour-power nor his means of production. In the capitalist mode of production, the worker owns his labour-power but not his means of production, and this defines capitalists and proletarian as two antagonist classes. In one word, what defines a mode of production is neither a type of technology and of division of labour, although they shape all social life, nor the social relations between classes, although they also structure social life, but a conjunction of these two conditions. It means that social life is not only structured by social factors, but also by technological ones,[136] and this thesis is indeed insightful for contemporary critical theory.

The conception of the modes of production leads to two possible readings of history. The first one is delineated in the preface of *A contribution to the critique of political economy*: the transition from one mode of production to another occurs when 'the material productive forces of society come into conflict with the existing relations of production (…) within the framework of which

134 This is one of the themes that makes possible to read Marx's political thought as paving the way to eco-socialism or green socialism or socialist ecology; see J.B. Foster, *Marx's Ecology. Materialism and Nature*, New York: Monthly Review Press, 2000.

135 T.W. Adorno, M. Horkheimer, *Dialectics of Enlightenment*, Stanford: Stanford University Press, 2002.

136 In Marx scholarship, some authors have tried to highlight, and probably overestimated, the technological factor in Marx conception of history; see notably, G. Cohen, *Karl Marx's Theory of History. A Defence*, Oxford: Clarendon Press, 2000.

they have operated hitherto'. This is the economic reading of history. But we have also noticed that a political revolution was necessary for this transition to occur. According to the second reading, which is a political reading of history, the class struggle between exploited and exploiting classes is the decisive factor of social evolution. This political dimension of the materialist conception of history is highlighted in the *Communist Manifesto*: 'The history of all hitherto existing society is the history of class struggles.'[137]

It is worth noting that the principles of the materialist conception of history, as presented in *The German Ideology*, the *Communist Manifesto* and the preface to *A contribution to the critique of political economy*, are only general principles that are intended to provide tools for empirical inquiries about past history and for the epistemological, sociological, and political self-reflection of the communist movement. As Engels will say later, in a letter to Conrad Schmidt dated 5 August 1880: 'our conception of history is above all a guide to study, not a lever for construction after the manner of the Hegelian.' Marx's materialist conception of history is a 'guide to study' and not a new philosophy of history or a fully elaborated theory. The only systematic theory of social evolution that he has elaborated on the basis of this guide to study is *Capital*, the book to which the rest of this part is devoted.

If Marx is still one of our contemporaries 200 years after his birth, it is notably because this masterpiece is one of the most profound analyses of the social dynamics that specifies the mode of production that is still shaping our societies, namely capitalism. *Capital* provides a definition of capitalism as the accumulation of capital and endless search for profit. This definition is still useful in order to understand that capitalism is not only a market economy, and is not only defined by the dynamics of endless commodification. *Capital* also provides a theory that can compete with mainstream economics and shed light on the latest evolution of capitalism.[138] Furthermore, it elaborates general distinctions that still have strong hermeneutic potential today: such as the distinction between formal and real subsumptions or that of absolute and relative surplus-value. The first distinction is intended to describe the dynamics in which social activities, and especially working activity, are not only instrumentalized by capitalist logics (formal subsumption) but restructured in order to become functional to the requisites of the production of surplus-value (real subsumption).[139] In other words, it describes the dynamics of integration of all

137 CW 6: 482.

138 See for instance G. Dumenil, D. Lévy, *The Crisis of Neoliberalism*, Harvard: Harvard University Press, 2013.

139 See "Results of the Immediate Process of Production", in *Capital I*, 1019–1038.

activities with the logic of the valorization of capital, or, to put it in Adornian terms, a tendency of capitalist societies to become 'systems', in the sense of a system unified by the dynamic of accumulation of capital.[140]

The distinction between absolute and relative surplus-value has another function. It describes two different modes of production of surplus-value, that is, two different modes of exploitation. Terminological clarifications are required on this particular point. According to Marx, the 'value' (as 'exchange value' and not 'use value') of a commodity corresponds to the quantity of labour that is socially required to produce it. 'Surplus-value' corresponds the 'surplus-labour', that is, the quantity of labour that exceeds 'necessary labour', or labour required to produce the same value as the value paid in wages. The term 'exploitation' denotes the fact that workers are compelled to work more than the working hours corresponding to the 'necessary labour'. Now, there are two different ways of producing surplus-labour and hence surplus-value. The first one consists in extending the working day. The surplus-value produced by this type of exploitation, corresponding to the first phase of capitalism, is labeled 'absolute surplus-value'. But indeed, this ways of producing surplus-value quickly meets its limits. There are physiological limits to the extension of the working day, and destroying the labour-power is not very efficient from an economic point of view. In order to produce more surplus-value, and also because of worker resistance against over-exploitation, a new type of exploitation emerges, in which the surplus-value is produced by a restriction of the quantity of working hours required to produce the value paid in wages. In other words, the growth of surplus-value is produced by a growth of productivity that results from technical progress and by reorganization of the labour process (or 'real subsumption').[141] If this distinction has not lost its heuristic power, it is notably because contemporary capitalism illustrates a return to absolute surplus-value: extension of the working day, blurring of the limits of the working day, delay of the legal age for retirement, and child work in the periphery of the world economy, all results in producing exploitation in extending the working hours, at the level of the working day and of working life as a whole.[142]

Notwithstanding, the relevance of *Capital* for contemporary social theory seems to be less acknowledged than the relevance of his conception of

140 See *Negative Dialectics*, Introduction.

141 *Capital I*, ch. 12.

142 On the implications of the transformations of contemporary capitalism for contemporary critical theory, see C. Dejours, J.-P. Deranty, E. Renault, N. Smith, *The Return of Work*, New-York: Columbia University Press, 2018.

philosophy and his accounts of the primacy of the practical. That is the reason why I will address, in what follows, three main objections that are often raised against *Capital* in contemporary critical theory: firstly, *Capital* would assume a theory of domination that is too simplistic; secondly, it would elaborate a theory of social evolution that is too deterministic and underestimates the role of political agency; and thirdly, it would wrongly consider that it is enough for social critique to rely upon a theory of the contradictions of the capitalist mode of production. Indeed, these objections also target the very principles of the materialist conception of history, but since this conception has never taken the form of a systematic theory in Marx, the only way to decide whether these objections are in general legitimate or not is to wonder whether they are convincing or not in so far as *Capital* is concerned.

Domination

Marx remains a central figure in contemporary debates about the relevance of the category of domination, and these debates still play a decisive role in contemporary critical theory. But usually, his approach to domination is subjected to criticisms. For instance, it has become commonplace to contrast the wrong assumptions of Marx's approach to domination with the accuracy of Foucauldian views on power. According to Deleuze's presentation of Foucault's idea, Marx reduces domination to a 'macro-power', exercised by entities such as the 'dominant classes' and their servant, the 'state', thus forgetting both the relational dimension of power as well as its rooting in the 'micro-powers' distributed throughout social life in its entirety.[143] Another frequent Foucauldian criticism of Marx's conception of power is that it assumes that the economic base of society is the cause of the relations of domination, while economic relations are also structured by power-relations. But in some texts, Foucault supports exactly the opposite views. In his conference "The Meshes of Power",[144] he points out that the relevance of the analysis of power proposed by Marx is threefold. First, this relevance stems from the fact that *Capital* discloses the heterogeneity of power relations in opposing the functioning of juridical-political power, functioning with reference to equality and liberty, and the processes at play in the workplaces, characterized by inequality and hierarchical constraints. Secondly, this relevance stems from the way in which *Capital* analyzes the diversity of the mechanisms of power that are at play in the workplaces – which is to

143 See the synthesis by G. Deleuze, *Foucault*, London: Continuum, 2006, 21–28. But indeed, it is also possible to read Marx with Foucault, see for instance J. Bidet, *Foucault avec Marx*, Paris: La Fabrique, 2014.

144 M. Foucault, "The Meshes of Power."

say, on the one hand, that Marx thought of the relations of production as structured by micro-powers, and on the other, that power-relations are constitutive of the economic basis of society. Thirdly, this relevance stems from the way in which *Capital* studies the history of these power-relations and of the technological devices they rely upon, a history that is explained in particular by the need to undermine workers' resistance. As Marx wrote in *Capital*: 'It would be possible to write a whole history of the inventions made since 1830 for the sole purpose of providing capital with weapons against working class revolt.'[145] In fact, Marx's theory of domination entails much more fruitful insights than usually acknowledged. It interconnects a conception of domination as class domination, that is, as structural domination or as macro-power, with a conception of domination exerted through specific interactions on the market and within the workplace. It also interconnects a conception of domination as relations between classes, at the macro level, and individuals, at the micro level, with a conception of domination as exerted by impersonal mechanisms such as economic constraints and technological devices. To begin with, let's try to clarify the very meaning given by Marx to the term 'domination'.

In Marx's texts, it seems that the term 'domination' (*Herrschaft*) invariably refers to a relationship of 'subordination' between individuals and groups (a subordinating-subordinated relationship, or *Über- und Unterordnung*, as Marx writes occasionally), a relationship marked by the 'constraint' (*Zwang*) by which individuals see their actions subjected, directly or indirectly, to the will of those to whom they are subordinated. This means that neither simple hierarchy, nor mere constraint, nor even the combination of the two, is enough to define domination. It also requires the addition of either the commandment of others (for example, in the wage relation), or submission to the interests of others (for example, economic mechanisms that constrain individuals to accept exploitative offers because of a survival constraint). Thus defined, domination concerns relations between individuals; however, relations of domination are carried out in the framework of relatively stable social structures. These latter structures contribute to the production and reproduction of class relations – in capitalism, relations between the class of proletarians and that of capitalists. Marx's originality is undeniable, then, to have referred relations of subordination and constraint between individuals to social relations cleaving the social world, between the ruling and dominated classes. But it equally resides in the fact, which he underlined, that the production and reproduction of these social relations of domination depend upon an entire panoply of economic mechanisms, upon processes of division of labour, and upon technological

145 *Capital I*, 563.

apparatuses, the effects of which unfold at the level of individual interactions. Lastly, it is to have underscored that the permanence of relations of domination presumes specific modes of legitimization and dissimulation.

The Marxian concept of domination doubtless has its center of gravity in the concept of class. As explained in the *Communist Manifesto*, history is invariably marked by a conflict between the dominant and dominated classes, the stake of which is the appropriation of the products of labour. As already noted in the last part, the specificity of capitalism resides, more particularly, in a simplification of this fundamental antagonism; in it, class struggle is gradually reduced to a confrontation between capitalists and proletarians. Marx's conception of domination, then, is based on the idea of class domination and is marked by the economic connotations of the Marxian concept of classes. Just as social classes are defined on the basis of ownership of the means of production and the products of labour, so too class domination is defined on the basis of exploitation. It would nevertheless be unfair to reproach Marx for having reduced domination to an economic phenomenon, since he underscores, notably in *The German Ideology*, the fact that class domination necessarily relies on political institutions (the state) and ideology. But it nevertheless remains true that, when they are broached, the forms of political and ideological domination (to say nothing of the forms of cultural, sexual and ethno-racial domination) are always thematized as moments subordinate to economic domination. The fact that this sounds too reductionist for all of those who have learned to take sex and race domination seriously, should not lead one to neglect to remember that many conceptions of sex or race domination have inherited much from Marx. For by grasping domination on the basis of social classes, Marx has been led to forge the concept of the social relationship of domination which has been so influential in critical sociology (in Bourdieu's for instance) and in feminist theories.[146]

The concept of the social relationship of domination implies that domination is irreducible to relations of dependency and constraint (between individuals and between groups), since the latter are part of a relationship between social positions that individuals are constrained to occupy. This relation subjects individuals to social groups and contributes to reproducing asymmetrical relations between these groups. As a social relationship, domination produces a specific type of subjectivation. Marx thus claims that the capitalist is merely the 'personification' of capital, in the same way that the worker is reduced to labour, as constructed in the social relationship capital/labour. To put it as in

146 See the volume coordinated by A. Bidet-Mordrel, *Les Rapports sociaux de sexe*, Paris: PUF, 2010.

the preface to *Capital*, individuals only enter into a relationship of domination as 'bearers of particular class-relations and interests and not as the singular individual responsible for relations whose creature he remains, socially speaking.'[147] To say that individuals are products of the social relationship of domination here means that the process of socialization constrains them to occupy, and to identify with, one of two positions in an asymmetrical relation, and that their views of the social world as well as their behaviors is deeply affected by this. Just as Marx is probably the first to have conceived domination as subjection (or 'personification'), so too he is probably the first to have thought of the permanence of domination via a theory of reproduction. The relationship of domination linking capitalists with proletarians is based, more particularly, on economic mechanisms that prohibit waged workers from surviving otherwise than by constantly renewing the wage relation. That is one of the particular aspects of what Marx calls 'simple reproduction', which is to say, the process by which the capitalist forever reproduces his own conditions.[148] This type of reproduction also defines a social relation of domination, be it achieved through economic constraints, as in Marx, or via social rituals, as in Goffman,[149] or via a symbolic violence, as in Bourdieu.[150]

In Marx, the concept of the social relationship of domination participates in a differentiated conception of domination. The capacity of the dominant to get the dominated to obey or to act in conformity with their interests can be explained not only by the direct constraints exerted through workplace sanctions (dismissal, fines, and salary deductions, etc.) and repression (the intermediary of state violence against resistance to domination), but equally by the indirect constraints that render sanctions and repression pointless, namely the objective, indirect constraints of economic processes and the organization of labour. Marx even seems to think that all of these indirect constraints play a more determinant role in capitalism than in previous modes of production. This is the sense of his saying that

> the capital-relation is a relation of compulsion, the aim of which is to extract surplus labour by extending labour time – it is a relation of compulsion that does not rest on personal relations of domination

147 *Capital I*, 92.

148 *Capital I*, 711–724.

149 E. Goffman, "The Arrangement between the Sexes", *Theory and Society*, Volume 4, Number 3, 1977, 301–331.

150 P. Bourdieu, *Pascalian Meditations*, Stanford: Stanford University Press, 2000, ch. 5.

> and dependence, but simply arises out of the difference in economic functions.[151]

Whence the oft-cited assertions, according to which, in capitalism, 'personal capacity is transformed into objective wealth' and 'personal independence [is] founded on objective (*sachlicher*) dependence.'[152] Whereas the slave or serf is caught in a relationship of personal dependency as regards the master or lord, capitalism is specified by 'objective dependency relations (…) in antithesis to those of personal dependence': 'individuals are now ruled by abstractions, whereas earlier they depended on one another.'[153] According to some influential authors of contemporary critical theory, who define themselves as Marxist inspired by Adorno and the tradition of Frankfurt critical theory, these latter quotes disclose what is most fundamentally original in Marx's conception of domination.[154] Marx would have contended that the subjection of individuals to capitalist social relations does not depend on the domination of specific social groups by others but on the domination of individuals by 'abstractions' and 'things'. In capitalist societies, social life is dominated by the abstraction of 'value', since an activity, a service of a good could not be recognized in its social worth unless it presents itself as having a monetary value that consists of an abstract commensurability between all activities, services, and goods. In capitalism, individuals are also dominated by things such as the technologies that structures their lives, and the means of subsistence over which they have lost all direct control. In other words, the concept of domination would have to be replaced by, or reformulated in terms of, alienation (by which is meant a situation in which humans are dominated by the products of their activity) or reification (by which is meant a situation where the value of the commodities seems to be disconnected from one's work and need and is only an actualization of an abstract idea of value). The problem which such types of interpretation is that if the Early Marx grounded his critical theory on the concept of alienation, at the time of the *Manuscripts of 1844*, this notion has

151 K. Marx, "Results of the Immediate Process of Production", 1021. See also, at 989: "In fact the rule of the capitalists over the workers is nothing but the rule of the independent conditions of labour over the worker, conditions that have made themselves independent of him".

152 K. Marx, *Grundrisse*, London: Penguin Books, 1973, 158.

153 *Grundrisse*, 164.

154 See for instance M. Postone, *Time, Labour, and Social Domination*, Cambridge, UK: Cambridge University Press, 1996.

lost its decisive role in the writings of the Mature Marx.[155] The notion of 'reification', which became a decisive concept of critical theory only after Lukacs's *History and Class Cousciousness* and is still at issue in contemporary debates,[156] plays an even less important role in Marx. It intervenes only in the part on the "Fetish character of the commodity", where Marx analyses the illusionary representation of value as a property that commodities possess in themselves and by themselves and is the reason why workers do not perceive value as an objectification of their own labor. Value is reified in so far as it appears as a thing and not as social labour. Conversely, the notion of class domination plays a decisive role in the writings of the Mature Marx. Far from bearing witness to a rejection of the problematics of domination, the quotes I am analyzing intend to specify the forms of domination in the capitalist mode of production, and they do not exclude the permanence or development of forms of personal domination and class domination. There is permanence of personal domination in the workplace, but these relations are mediated by technological constraints, such as the rhythm of the machine to which the worker must obey. There is also permanence of class domination, but it is mediated by the economic constraints that compel workers to sell their work-power to the capitalists.

In capitalist societies, personal domination and class domination are not only mediated by impersonal constraints; they are also backed up and reinforced by these constraints. But this doesn't mean that the capitalist domination deprives workers of all agency and capacity to resist domination. Paradoxically, Marx considered that subjection is never complete except on the side of those who occupy the position of domination, and this is what led him to depict waged work as a critical point of view on domination as well as a source of 'rebellion'. The following quote illustrates what I alluded to in the previous part when I mentioned the legitimation potential of the social position of the ruling classes and critical potential of the social position of the dominated classes:

> To that extent, the worker stands on a higher plane than the capitalist from the outset, since the latter has his roots in the process of alienation and finds absolute satisfaction in it whereas right from the start

---

155 A point that has been made notably by the Althusserian school notably in *Reading Capital*.

156 For a contemporary use of this concept, see A. Honneth, *Reification. A New Look at an Old Idea*, Oxford: Oxford University Press, 2008.

> the worker is a victim who confronts it as a rebel and experiences it as a process of enslavement (*Knechtungsprocess*).[157]

In other words, Marx's conception of structural domination is associated with a conception of the structural possibility of critique and resistance, and with a necessity for structural domination to justify itself against criticism, as well as a necessity to control this resistance. What is at stake in this conception of domination, critique, and resistance can be made explicit by comparing Marx's views with the sociology of domination elaborated by Bourdieu. In reference to the Weberian idea that no relationship of domination can subsist without being accompanied by principles that make it legitimate in the eyes of those subjected to it,[158] Bourdieu, on the contrary, maintains that the 'recognition of legitimacy is not, as Weber supposed, a free act of lucid consciousness: it is rooted in the immediate agreement between the incorporated structures, turned into practical schemes … and the objective structures.'[159] The question at issue could be presented as follows: is the permanence of domination explained by processes that legitimate it (Weber) or, on the contrary, by processes that dissimulate it in the eyes of those who endure it and by the same token render its legitimization pointless (Bourdieu)? Marx's answer seems to combine both options. On the one hand, he contends, in *The German Ideology*, that the dominant classes tend to produce ideas that justify their domination and that contribute to imposing it on the whole of society. It is in this sense that he can define ideology at once as the ideas of the dominant class, the ideas of its domination, and the dominant ideas, as noted in the next part. But, on the other hand, he also underscores the importance of processes that dissimulate the veritable nature of domination. On this point, it could be added that Marx's originality is to conceive this concealment in terms of the 'mystification' produced by the positions occupied in social relations, where Bourdieu conceives of it in terms of the 'misrecognition' produced by the adaptation of habitus to relations of domination, that is to say by subjection.[160] For Marx, domination is not only based on ideological legitimation, but also on mystifying illusions, notably on those 'fetishist' illusions which arise from the way in which value and our social relations mediated by value appear to us in the very

157 "Results of the Immediate Process of Production", 990.

158 M. Weber, *Economy and Society*, Berkeley: California University Press, 1978, 212.

159 P. Bourdieu, *Pascalian Meditations*, 178.

160 For a confrontation between Marx and Bourdieu on this point, see M. Burawoy, *Conversations with Bourdieu. The Johannesburg Moment*, Johannesburg: Wits University Press, 2012, ch. VIII.

process of social action.[161] It is through the concepts of commodity fetishism and what one could call machine fetishism that he notably developed these ideas. Just as the forms that value takes in market interactions tend to make relations of domination between the capitalist and the waged worker appear as natural and necessary since it is based on the exchange value of work-power and exchange value appears as a natural relation, so too the conditions of labour in large-scale industry tend to make machines appear as the source of value and labour as an activity that should be put at their service (an activity that, by this fact, is legitimately controlled and monitored by machines).[162]

Agency

As noted at the beginning of this part, the materialist conception of history seems to elaborate two distinct if not opposite conceptions of history: one that conceives history as an economic process, the other as a political process. A first sight, in *Capital*, only the first model plays a decisive role, and Marx's masterpiece is often criticized for this very reason. It would propose a too economistic interpretation of history and would be in contradiction to the conception of history as the history of class struggles, as well as with the political project of a self-emancipation of the proletariat. These critical readings of Marx, charging him for having underestimated the role of the political struggles, if not to have denied agency to proletarians, are usually based on two interpretative lines. The first one depicts Marx as a determinist and economistic theoretician of social evolution. The second one consists in reading *Capital* as a theory of the progressive undermining of the resistance of the proletarians. Gramsci has already, in his article "The Revolution against 'Capital'" (1917), contended that *Capital* elaborates a conception of social evolution in which the class struggles and worker resistances do not play a decisive role. The social evolution of capitalist societies would be solely governed by the necessary laws expressive of the structural contradictions of the economic basis of these societies. Some passages of the preface to *Capital* seem to provide confirmation to such an interpretation, for Marx himself has pointed out that:

161 On the double level of justification, see E. Renault, "L'idéologie comme légitimation et comme description", *Actuel Marx*, n° 43, 2008, 80–95.

162 Marx, *Capital I*, 163. On the fetishism attached to the 'mystification of capital', and on its intensification with the transition to large scale industry, see Marx, "Results of the Immediate Process of Production", 989, 1008–9, 1021, 1024. A study of the evolution of the Marxian analysis of 'machines' is given in A.M. Wendling, *Karl Marx on Technology and Alienation*, Basingstoke, UK: PalgraveMacmillan, 2009.

> Even when a society has begun to track down the natural laws of its movement – and it is the ultimate aim of this work to reveal the economic law of motion of modern society – it can neither leap over the natural phases of its development nor remove them by decree.[163]

According to the other interpretative line, Marx would have described the development of capitalism as a gradual subjugation of worker's resistance, and would have depicted mature capitalism as a set of economic and social processes that makes social and political resistances impossible.[164] Here again, some passages seem to support this reading:

> The advance of capitalist production develops a working class which by education, tradition and habit looks upon the requirements of that mode of production as self-evident natural laws. The organization of the capitalist process of production, once it is fully developed, breaks down all resistance.[165]

But on closer reading, it appears that Marx has neither thought of the 'laws of the capitalist production' as 'necessary' laws, nor of the capitalist social relations as an 'iron cage' in the Weberian sense of the term.[166] A first point to note is that Marx has explicitly criticized classical political economy for having searched its methodological model in the Newtonian mechanics. Two reasons make the laws of capitalist production distinct from the laws of motion or gravitation. Firstly, the laws studied by political economy are historical and not natural laws. Secondly, these laws are not deterministic in the same sense as mechanical laws. In *Capital*, the laws of the evolution of capitalist societies are conceived of as 'tendential laws'. They are deterministic in so far as they describe a tendency that necessarily operates. But they are non-deterministic in so far as the ways in which these tendencies operate depends on 'counteracting factors'. For instance, the counteracting factors of the law of the tendential fall of the rate of profit are the following: a higher degree of exploitation, a reduction of wages, an increasing unemployment, a development of international

163 *Capital I*, 92.

164 This reading is instantiated, notably in M. Postone, *Time, Labour, and social domination* and P. Dardot, C. Laval, *Marx, Prénom: Karl*, Paris: Gallimard, 2012.

165 *Capital I*, 899.

166 See M. Weber, *The Protestant Ethic and the Spirit of Capitalism*, New York: Charles Scribner's Sons, 1950, 181.

trade, etc. All of these counteracting factors can provisionally slow down or even stop the fall of the profit rate.[167]

The idea of 'tendential law' entails a very original conception of law, from an epistemological point of view, as well as from the points of view of social ontology and theory of history. From an epistemological point of view, its function is to explain the social evolution rather than forecasting this evolution. Far from simply describing an empirical regularity, tendential law explains social evolution by making explicit the economic dynamics that are structuring this evolution, and it also explains how they are at work in this evolution. The concept of tendential law elaborates an original theoretical model in which, on the one hand, some forces have an explanatory power since they are necessarily at work, but on the other hand, these forces always act in conjunction with a plurality of other factors, some of which counteract the effects produced by these forces. From an ontological point of view, the concept of tendential law is dependent on a vision of the social not only as a set of structures and relations, but also of processes that are not only the actualization of the contradictions of permanent structures and relations, but also continuous transformations of permanent structures and relations. In other words, the ontological assumptions of Marx's theory of tendential law belongs to a processual ontology according to which there is a primacy of processes over structures and relations.[168] And from the point of view of the theory of history, the conception of tendential law entails a vision of social evolution being not only subjected to the development of permanent principles, and not having the homogeneity that makes it susceptible to being described by the traditional concept of law, but also characterized by the emergence of the new.[169]

It is worth noting that *Capital* is a theory of processes. Its general contention is that capitalism is to be conceived of as a set of processes, with process being defined, in the words used in a note for the French edition, as 'a development considered in all of its real conditions.'[170] The titles of the three books composing *Capital* are respectively, 'the process of production of capital', 'the process of circulation of capital', and 'the process of capitalist production as a whole'. And in each book, many processes are studied. For instance, in the first part of Book I, the exchange of commodity is clearly conceived of as 'a development

167 *Capital III*, 339–348.

168 On this primacy, see E. Renault, "Critical Theory and Processual Social Ontology".

169 Adorno has insisted on these dimensions of Marx's concept of 'Tendenz' that makes it irreducible to a simple 'trend'; see his lessons *Philosophische Elemente einer Theorie der Gesellschaft*, Frankfurt: Suhrkamp, 2008, p. 37–40.

170 K. Marx, *Le Capital. Livre 1, tome 1*. Paris 1978, S. 181.

considered in all of its real conditions'. The theory of the 'process of exchange' (the title of chapter 2) presupposes a theory of the relations between use value and exchange value (chapter 1 a & b) as well as a theory of the relations between the relative and equivalent forms of value (chapter 1 c), but also a theory of the representation of the value that drives the social agents in exchanges (chapter 1 d: fetishism) and a theory of their mutual expectations in their interactions (beginning of chapter 2, which I will analyze in the next section). It is also worth noting that this processual conception of capitalism is incompatible with a conception of capitalism as a set of permanent social structures or as an essence gradually actualizing itself in its purest form. Indeed, there is a tendency in contemporary critical theory to speak of contemporary capitalism as 'pure' or 'absolute' capitalism. But far from being in tune with such an essentialist conception of capitalism, Marx supports a historical conception of capitalism as constantly attempting to find new solutions to its structural contradictions. To put it like the preface of *Capital*: 'the present society is not a solid crystal, but an organism capable of change, and constantly engaged in a process of change.'[171]

Until now, I have considered the criticism of Marx depicting him as reducing social evolution to determinist laws. But the reproach is also that he would have thought of the evolution of capitalist societies in terms purely economical, without taking the role of social and political agency into account. Again, the criticism is unfair. There is no doubt that Marx in *Capital* wants to produce a theory of the economic dynamics that define capitalism as such. It is also true that in this context, social agents is conceived of as the 'personification' of economic categories, as noted in the previous section of this part. In this respect, it is not surprising that social and political agency do not come to the fore. They nevertheless play a twofold role. The first concerns the fact that the workers struggle in order to shorten the working day and to increase wages. These struggles have an impact on the factors that counteract the tendential law of the decrease of the profit rate, and they compel capitalists to invent new ways to produce surplus-value. Hence the metamorphosis of the production process that consists in the shift from manufacture to large scale industry, or the shift from absolute to relative surplus-value, hence the fact that 'it would be possible to write a whole history of the inventions made since 1830 for the sole purpose of providing capital with weapons against working class revolt.'[172]

171 *Capital I*, 93.
172 *Capital I*, 563.

Social and political agency also play a role in the theory of the transition from capitalism to communism. Among the immanent laws of capitalist production that are studied in *Capital*, some are presented as 'antagonistic' laws. This is the case with what Marx presents in chapter 25 as the general law of capitalist production: the law of the production of relative overpopulation (that is structural unemployment), and the consequent effects of impoverishment. The term 'antagonism' is then used to describe the fact that the law of capitalist accumulation defines a contradiction that is not economic or functional, but socio-political. The law of centralization of capital, formulated in chapter 25 of Book I, and that of the tendency of the rate of profit to fall formulated in the third section of Book III, describe only economic or functional contradictions. They describe the mechanisms by which the development of capitalism destroys its own presuppositions, namely the private ownership of the means of production (the 'expropriation of the usurpers'[173]) and the production of surplus-value. The law of relative overpopulation, that is, the law which describes the production of structural unemployment, is of a different nature. It describes a process that contributes to the reproduction by capitalism of its own conditions. In other words, it describes a functional necessity rather than a functional contradiction. The existence of a relative overpopulation, or of a reserve army of the unemployed, makes it possible to exert a pressure on the wage, which makes it possible to counteract the decline in the rate of profit. In this respect, it responds to a functional need. Nevertheless, it also defines a contradiction, a contradiction of a social and political nature. It keeps the working class in a misery which transforms it into an antagonistic social class and thus creates the conditions for a political struggle against the capitalist mode of production. Marx writes in chapter 25:

> In proportion as capital accumulates, the situation of the worker, be his payment high or low, must grow worse. (…) Accumulation of wealth at one pole is, therefore, at the same time accumulation of misery, the torment of labour, slavery, ignorance, brutalization and moral degradation at the opposite pole, i.e. on the side of the class that produces its own product as capital. The antagonistic character of capitalist accumulation has been enunciated in various forms by political economists.[174]

173 *Capital I*, 930.

174 *Capital I*, 799. See also page 798: 'The relative mass of industrial reserve army increases with the potential energy of wealth. But the greater this reserve army in proportion to the active labour-army, the greater is the mass of consolidated surplus population, whose misery is in inverse ratio to the amount of torture is has to undergo in the form of labour.

In this excerpt, the notion of antagonism expresses social antagonism, a 'class antagonism' to use a formula that occurs several times in *Capital*, and which was already already used in the *Communist Manifesto* where the term was obviously taken up from Saint-Simonism, and more particularly from *The exposition of the doctrine of Saint-Simon*,[175] which presented past history as that of the antagonist of the workers and idlers and that of the exploitation of man by man. The term antagonism, like that of exploitation, belongs to the Saint-Simonian vocabulary of Marx, and like in the Saint-Simonians, it has an immediately social and political significance. As recalled at the beginning of this part, in Marx's materialist conception of history, it is on the basis of class antagonism that politics is approached. One finds the trace of this approach to politics in the use *Capital* makes of the term antagonism. And it is worth noting that in the conclusion of *Capital* Book I, it is precisely this type of antagonism that will explain the transition from capitalism to communism.

> Along with the constant decrease in the number of capitalist magnates, (...) the mass of misery, oppression, slavery and degradation and exploitation grows; but with this there is also growth of revolt of the working class, a class constantly increasing in numbers, and trained, united and organized by the very mechanism of the capitalist process of production. The monopoly of capital becomes a fetter upon the mode of production which has flourished alongside and under it. The centralization of the means of production and the socialization of labour reach a point at which they become incompatible with their capitalist integument. This integument is burst asunder. The knell of capitalist private property sounds. The expropriators are expropriated.[176]

This passage is interesting in many ways. On the one hand, it presents the immanent tendencies of capitalist production as tendencies which make the communist mode of production emergent within the capitalist mode of production: the centralization of capital and the socialization of labor prepare communism. Furthermore, as noted in Book III, shareholders' firms and

---

The more extensive, finally, the pauperized sections of the working class and the industrial reserve army, the greater is official pauperism. *This is the absolute general law of capitalist accumulation*. Like all other laws, it is modified in its working by many circumstances, the analysis of which does not concern us here.'

175 *Doctrine de Saint-Simon*, Paris: Au bureau de l'organisateur, 1829, http://gallica.bnf.fr/ark:/12148/bpt6k85469w.

176 *Capital I*, 929.

cooperatives are negations of the private ownership of the means of production within the mode of production based on the private ownership of the means of production.[177] On the other hand, this passage connects the idea of the immanent economic evolution of capitalism towards communism, due to its tendential laws, with the idea of a political action of the proletariat. This interconnection is expressed in the double sense given to the idea of expropriation of expropriators: it refers both to an immanent law (that of the centralization of capital) and to a political act: the expropriators are expropriated by the working class. Finally, this text emphasizes the twofold origin of the struggles of the proletariat: on the one hand, a motivation (the 'growth of revolt'), and on the other hand, the social processes that allow the feelings of revolt to be shared and organized: the working class is 'trained, united, and organized by the very mechanism of the capitalist production process', notably by the constitution of large scale industry and the formation of trade-unions.

We are very far from the idea that economic laws would in themselves lead to communism and just as far from the themes of a capitalism that breaks all resistance. Indeed, Marx has written, as quoted below, that 'fully developed [capitalism], breaks down all resistance'. But this sentence is located in a passage where Marx refers to the fact that wage labour has become a habit for workers when societies have become capitalist. It is simply a fact that for workers, it has become self-evident that waged work is the only way to earn their living. But this quote does not mean that waged workers have seen their resistances broken down. On the contrary, in a quite Foucauldian way, Marx has tried to show that the power-relations embedded in the employer/worker relationship generates resistances on the part of the workers. The first appearance of the worker in the order of exposition of *Capital* defines it by a disposition to insubordination in the form of reluctance. The worker 'holds back, like someone who has carried his own hide from the market and now has nothing to expect but – a tanning.'[178] Marx later describes the different forms this insubordination can take, from passive resistance to open political struggle. These two types of insubordination play an equally important role in chapter 10, devoted to the working day, and especially in its long section 6, entitled "The struggle for a normal working day. Laws for a compulsory limitation of working

177 *Capital III*, 572: 'Capitalist joint-stock companies as much as cooperative factories should be viewed as transition forms from the capitalist mode of production to the associated one, simply that in the one case the opposition is abolished in a negative way, and in the other in a positive way'.

178 *Capital I*, p. 280.

hours. The English factory legislation of 1833–1864". Marx writes in particular, with regard to the abolition of the 10-hour law in 1850:

> But this apparently decisive victory of capital was immediately followed by a counter-stroke. So far, the workers have offered a resistance which was passive, though inflexible and unceasing. They now protested in Lancashire and Yorkshire in threatening meetings. (…) The factory inspectors urgently warned the government that class antagonisms had reached an unheard-of degree of tension (…). Under these circumstances, it came to a compromise between manufacturers and men, given the seal of parliamentary approval in the supplementary Factor Act of 5 August 1850.[179]

The worker is not characterized here by consent to domination, but by 'resistance which was passive, though inflexible and unceasing.' Moreover, Marx emphasizes that the transition from manufacte to large-scale industry, that is to say, the emergence of fully developed capitalism, far from creating a docile proletariat, transforms worker insubordination into a direct struggle of the proletariat against the domination to which it is subjected. While the worker, at the beginning of this new phase of capitalism, revolts against the machine, once he resigns himself to working at the machine's command, he begins to understand that behind the machine, it is to the demand for the valorization of capital that he is enslaved. In chapter 15, "Machinery and large-scale industry", section 5 is devoted to "The struggle between worker and machine". Referring to the Luddite movement, Marx points out that:

> It took time and experience before the worker learnt to distinguish between machinery and its employment by capital, and therefore to transfer their attacks from the material instruments of production to the form of society which utilizes those instruments.[180]

Later in the same chapter, Marx explains that the transformation of manufacture into large scale industry has been a decisive factor for this learning process. It made the capitalist logic of the valorization of capital easier to perceive, as well as the seriousness of its damaging effects for the working class:

---

179 *Capital I*, 405.

180 *Capial I*, 554–555.

> [Large-scale industry] destroys both the ancient and the transitional forms behind which the dominion of capital is still hidden, and replaces them with a dominion which is direct and unconcealed. By doing this it also generalizes the direct struggle against its rule.[181]

Marx's argument seems intended to prove that great industry, far from breaking resistance, is the occasion for an increase in the workers' combativeness. On the one hand, Marx emphasizes that the victories of the proletariat, as regards the limits of the working day, contribute to strengthening its struggles. On the other hand, he insists that the concentration of the proletariat in big plants allows it to organize itself and engage in a process of collective learning which makes its struggles both more effective and more lasting. Definitely, Marx's point is that capitalism is far from breaking down the workers' resistance. On the contrary, the most developed form of capitalism reinforces the struggles of the proletariat, and conversely, weakens the power of resistance of capital, as we see from the following excerpt from Chapter 10, which anticipates the conclusion of the book:

> It will be easily understood that after the factory magnates had resigned themselves and submitted to the inevitable, capital's power of resistance gradually weakened, while at the same time the working class's power of attack grew with the number of his allies in those social layers not directly interested in the question. Hence the comparatively rapid progress since 1860.[182]

Normativity and Critique

Another criticism often raised against *Capital* is that it assumes a functionalist theory according to which social norms are nothing but forms of social justification and dissimulations of dominations and injustices. This reproach is often associated with a criticism of his implicit model of social critique. Having reduced normative principles to ideology, and social norms to factors of social reproduction, he would have been obliged to ground his own social criticism on a theory of the contradictions of capitalism. This model of immanent critique, identifying social criticism with theory of the social contradictions, would be suffering from a normative deficit and would be incapable of

181 *Capital I*, 635.
182 *Capital I*, 409.

capturing the normative content of the struggles of the proletariat.[183] I have contended in the last part that Marx is not so much rejecting all normative accounts of worker resistances than rejecting all attempts to orient these resistances in reference to normative principles external to them. But the question at issue does not concern Marx's writings in general; it concerns specifically *Capital*. This question can be phrased in following terms: is it true that the role of normative principles in social life is denied in Marx's masterpiece and that social critique is articulated without any normative reference point?

The best way to answer this question is to refer to the passages in which Marx describes the norms of markets and the workers' struggles concerning the labour market, namely, the struggles concerning the price (wage) and the use (working hours) of the labour-force commodity. To begin with, it is worth noting that Marx does not consider the market only from a functionalist point of view – as a social sphere (the sphere of circulation) contrasted with another social sphere (the sphere of production) with both of them being dependent in various ways – but also as a set of social practices. Market does not mean only the transformation of value into prices and circulation of commodities but also social practices since 'commodities cannot themselves go to market and perform exchange in their own right.'[184] It is also useful to recall that Marx assumes that capitalist markets are regulated by rules of equality and freedom: market exchanges are mediated by (explicit or implicit) contracts that presuppose the equality and freedom of the contractors: at the beginning of chapter 2, it is written that on the market, individuals relate to each other freely and equally.[185] Marx adds on same page of chapter 2 that market functioning presupposes another normative condition: since the exchange is a free relation and since it is an exchange between equal values, the only reason to exchange is to substitute a commodity one needs for a commodity one does not need.[186] This principle of mutual usefulness is not to be identified with a principle of

183 For this type of criticism, see for instance A. Honneth, "Die Moral im 'Kapital'. Versuch einer Korrektur der Marxschen Ökonomiekritik", in *Nach Marx, Philosophie, Kritik, Praxis*, edited by R. Jaeggi and D. Loïck, Frankfurt: Suhrkamp 2013, 350–363.

184 *Capital I*, 178.

185 Exchange is an interaction that requires that owners 'recognize each other as owners of private property' (*Capital I*, 178). When Marx adds 'this juridical relation, whose form is the contract, whether as part of a developed legal system or not that, is a relation between two wills which mirrors the economic relation', he is not putting the ideological dimension of the legal conditions of exchanges in the fore. Rather, he is elaborating a phenomenology of interactions through social roles: 'the persons exist for one another merely as representatives and hence owner, of commodities'.

186 *Capital I*, 179.

solidarity. The Durkeimian identification of the social division of labour with social solidarity[187] loses its relevance in the capitalist markets where the wealth produced appears as an alien and oppressive power that becomes an obstacle to the satisfaction of the needs of the workers. Moreover, the competition that makes capitalist markets specific, in contrast with pre-capitalist markets, tends to destroy solidarity, and this tendency is all the more powerful on the labour market in the situation of unemployment (or 'relative surplus-population'). Indeed, solidarity still exists in the social behavior of market participants, but it is only the social antagonism between capitalists and proletarians that generates new form of solidarities: one the one hand, solidarity between workers in their attempt to balance the destructive effects that competition among themselves produces on their living conditions,[188] on their resistances and struggles, and on the other hand, solidarity between capitalists in their attempt to increase the average rate of profit. Markets *in general* are characterized by a principle of mutual usefulness, but not of solidarity, for capitalist markets, far from producing 'organic solidarity', are specified by a type of competition that undermines solidarity.

Notwithstanding, Marx's account of freedom, equality, and mutual usefulness as market principles entails a positive account of the markets in general and also of capitalist markets: they enable individuals to choose what they need and also the types of exchanges that will help them to satisfy their needs. But there is something specific in the capitalist labor market, and it is only with regard to this type of market that the three normative principles of market freedom, equality, and mutual usefulness become problematic and are mentioned ironically:

> The sphere of circulation or commodity exchange, within whose boundaries the sale and purchase of labour-power goes on, is in fact a very Eden of the innate rights of man. It is the exclusive real of Freedom, Equality, Property and Bentham.[189]

187 E. Durkheim, *The Division of Labor in Society*, New York: Free Press, 1997.

188 *Capital I*, 793: "the workers learn the secret of why it happens that the more they work, the more alien wealth they produce, and the more the productivity of their labour increases, the more does their very function as a means of production becomes precarious; (...) they discover that the degree of intensity of the competition amongst themselves depends wholly on the pressure of the relative surplus population ; (...) by setting up trade unions, etc. they try to organize planned co-operation between the employed and the unemployed in order to obviate or to weaken the ruinous effects of the natural law of capitalist production on their class".

189 *Capital I*, 280.

In this particular case, the criticism of the market principles of freedom, equality, and mutual usefulness is based on three separate arguments. The first one concerns the fact that the freedom of workers is only *formal*. The *Manifesto* has already highlighted the fact that this freedom is only the freedom of participating in a social competition that cannot be a means of self-realization since the work offered on the labour market 'has lost all individual character, and, consequently, all charm for the workman. He becomes an appendage of the machine, and it is only the most simple, most monotonous, and most easily acquired knack, that is required of him.'[190] Marx contrasts merely negative, or formal freedom of choice, with a positive freedom that demands that work be 'a means to widen, to enrich, to promote the existence of the labourer.'[191] In *Capital*, this contrast is articulated through the idea that the waged worker is free in a 'double sense': free of being no longer possessed as a means of production (such as slaves or serfs); and free in the sense of being deprived or detached of any production means.[192] It is worth noting that in this context, Marx is not saying that the freedom in the first sense has no worth. Rather, he acknowledges this worth but adds that it is only one side of the medal. His point is that the progress regarding freedom as freedom of choice on the labour market is balanced by a structural impossibility of converting this negative freedom into a positive one:

> The historical movement which changes the producers into wage-labourers appears, on the one hand, as their emancipation from serfdom and from the fetters of the guilds, and it is this aspect of the movement which alone exists for our bourgeois historians. But, on the other hand, these newly freed men became the sellers of themselves only after they had been robbed of all their own means of production and all the guaranties of existence afforded by the old feudal arrangements.[193]

Here, the principle of freedom on the labour market is not depicted as ideological *by itself*, but only as being possibly interpreted in an ideological way when this negative freedom only is taken into consideration and not also the structural impossibility of positive freedom. Marx acknowledges that this negative

190 CW 6, 490.

191 CW 6, 499.

192 *Capital I*, 874: 'Free workers are therefore free from, unencumbered by, any means of production of their own.'

193 *Capital I*, 875.

freedom should be conceived of as the 'positive aspect of waged labour',[194] without considering that this positive aspect is enough to give legitimacy to capitalist markets. He adds two arguments that give ideological dimensions to the very normative principles of the labour market.

The first one relates to the *dissimulation* of the structural inequality and domination that defines the relationship between capitalists and proletarians as a social relationship of production. On the labour market, this specific social relationship takes the phenomenal form of a free, equal, and useful interaction, a phenomenal form that dissimulates the fact that the exchange of labour-force for wage is based on a structural inequality (only some are in possession of means of production) and on a structural lack of freedom: for those who are deprived of means of production, and whose wage remains minimal, exchange is based on the constraint for survival rather than on freedom. As a consequence, it is not only the principles of freedom and equality, but also that of reciprocal utility that loses its normative value. As was the case with the theory of fetishism, the ideological dimension attached to the principles of the labour market consists here in a cognitive effect generated by the market: market as the phenomenal form of something that has reality outside of the market, as a phenomenal form that is an *illusion*.

The second ideological dimension regards the *legitimation* of the domination that operates in the work place. Then the ideological dimension no longer relates to freedom, equality, and mutual usefulness as *general forms of market exchanges*, but to the *specific form of the labour contract* as a contract of subordination. Its specificity is that the freedom of contracting, which has reality within the sphere of circulation, reverses into domination the working activity within the work place – where domination means not only obeying another will, but also being forced to spend surplus work.[195] Here the ideological dimension of the normative principles of the labour market no longer amounts to cognitive deficit. Rather, it relates to the fact that the principles of market interactions (freedom, equality, and mutual usefulness) and the principle of productive interactions (production of surplus-value through constraints) are heterogeneous and contradictory, even though the former gives justification to the latter through the labour contract.

But even if these principles have ideological dimensions, their use is not necessarily ideological. At the beginning of the chapter on the working day, Marx lets a worker speak and claims that the norms of freedom, equality, and mutual usefulness should be understood in such a way that the working day

194 CW 6, 436–437.

195 *Capital I*, 280.

should be restricted. Far from criticizing this use of market principles as ideological, Marx highlights its legitimacy:

> The peculiar nature of the commodity sold implies a limit to its consumption by the purchaser, and the workers maintains his right as a sellers when he wishes to reduce the working day to a particular normal length. (…) There is here therefore an antinomy, or right against right, both equally bearing the seals of the law of exchanges. Between equal rights, force decides.[196]

What follows from these comments is that despite their ideological dimension, the principles of the labour market do not lose all normative value. They could ground the legitimate claims that are raised by this worker in order to regulate the domination to which he is subjected – the labour contract being something that is constituted in market interactions but nevertheless impacts domination in the work places. The principles of the labour market could lead to market regulations as well as to work place regulations, but indeed, they lose their critical dimension when what is at stake is no longer the regulation but the radical transformation of the very functioning of capitalist markets and relations of production.

It is in this latter respect that Proudhon and other French socialists are wrong when they ground the project of abolishing exploitation in the norms of freedom and equality in exchanges. The problem is not only that these norms already structure market exchanges, so that one hardly sees how they could lead to something more than regulations of capitalist markets. The problem is also that capitalist exploitation is something other than forced work and robbery, so that the claim for more justice in exchanges misses the target. The target should rather be the structural conditions of exploitation, that is, the social relationship of production between proletarians and capitalists; and it should also be the actual form of exploitation in the sphere of production, in other words, the power relations that underpin the extraction of surplus-labour.

The purpose of the preceding remarks was to show that Marx's critique of capitalist markets is much more complex and multilayered as usually acknowledged. As a conclusion, let's try to locate it, more generally, in the ongoing debates about social critique. Here again, Marx could be considered as promoting a complex model of social critique in comparison to which the diverse positions that frame the contemporary discussion seem somehow one-sided.

---

196 *Capital I*, 344.

Regarding the *types* of critique, one could distinguish: 1) a critique of first-order social pathologies relating to the lack of efficiency of market competition and its ruinous effects on the workers' condition; 2) a critique of second-order social pathologies involving on the one hand a critique of ideology and on the other hand a critique of the undermining of social resources, such as networks of solidarity.

By social pathology I mean a type of social problem that doesn't relate to injustice, that is, to illegitimate inequalities, but to social settings that tend to damage individual and social life.[197] Markets could be considered as socially pathological in so far as some structural tendencies (periodicity of crises and pauperization) make them unable to satisfy social needs. Now, an institution can be described as participating in a second-order pathology when the way in which it impacts on social life generates obstacles to the resolution of social problems, be they social injustices or first-order social pathology.[198] Capitalist markets could be considered as social pathological in this sense in so far as they generate *cognitive* and *practical* problems that are obstacles to the resolution of their first-order social pathological dimension. On the cognitive side, the theory of the 'fetishism of the commodity' indicates that markets generate the illusion that their functioning relies upon natural laws and therefore cannot be modified. On the practical side, competition in the labor market undermines the old professional solidarities and generates another obstacle to the resolution of capitalist social pathologies: an obstacle that relates to the social conditions of collective mobilization. Hence, one could say that capitalist markets are criticized for their lack of efficiency, for the pauperization and cyclic crises that are generated by the competition between capitalists (first-order pathology) and for their negative effects on the cognitive and practical conditions that enable collective action to face social problems (second-order pathology).

Regarding the *norms* of the critique, one could distinguish: 1) a normative functionalism: markets are legitimate only insofar as they remain moments of social metabolism, that is insofar as they remain subordinated to an organic division of labour, or in other words, as far as they are actualizing relations

197 See A. Honneth, "Pathologies of the Social: The Past and Present of Social Philosophy", in *Disrespect: The Normative Foundations of Critical Theory*. Cambridge, UK: Polity Press, 2007, 3–48.

198 I'm distinguishing first order and second order pathologies while C. Zurn defines 'social pathologies' as 'second-order' social disorder; C. Zurn, "Social Pathologies As Second-Order Disorders", in *Axel Honneth: Critical Essays. With a Reply by Axel Honneth*, edited by D. Petherbridge, Dordrecht: Brill, 2011, 345–370.

of solidarity between the various social groups involved in the social division of labour; and 2) a reinterpretation of the meaning of equality, freedom, and mutual usefulness as fundamental norms: against the restricted meaning of market equality, freedom, and mutual usefulness, one should promote a conception of positive freedom and a primacy of the satisfaction of social needs over the rule of equality.[199] One could say that capitalist markets are criticized because they are reduced to means of accumulation of capital at the expense of the satisfaction of the need of the working class. They are criticized also because they are institutionalizing the restricted conception of freedom, equality, and mutual usefulness.

Regarding the *form* of the critique, it seems that Marx's critique of capitalist markets belongs neither to external critique (the critique of ideology makes it impossible to refer to universal and trans-historical norms), nor to immanent critique (it is not enough to refer to the meaning that capitalist societies associate to freedom, equality, and usefulness as economic, social, and political norms). Rather, the critique of capitalist markets relates to three models: The first model is a model in which social criticism is thought of as the self-reflective moment of social struggles. What is at stake in such a form of social criticism is to think of markets and production from the point of view of the workers' resistance against the degradation of their living conditions and from the point of view of their hope in a transformation of alienated work into emancipated work. The second model is a model of 'disclosing critique'[200] in which what is at stake is to give due consideration and accurate knowledge to what is dissimulated by the market functioning (work as the origin of value and exploitation as a social relationship of production). The third model is a model in which social critique needs to take into account the fact that the social world is differentiated into various social spheres ruled by specific principles of interaction. Just as freedom and equality could be actualized in the political sphere without being actualized in the social spheres, as highlighted by the early Marx, what is true in the sphere of circulation could be false in the sphere of production.

199 I'm referring here to the passage of the *Critique of Gotha Program* that has been quoted at the end of part 2.

200 On the notion of 'disclosing critique', and its echoes in Adorno, see A. Honneth, "The Possibility of a Disclosing Critique of Society: The Dialectic of Enlightenment in Light of Current Debates in Social Criticism", *Constellations*, Volume 7, Issue 1, 2000, 116–127.

Conclusion

The reading of Marx that has been delineated in the previous parts is influenced by Frankfurt critical theory, mainly by Adorno who was one of its founders,[201] but also by its latest developments. As a conclusion, I would like to shed light on the uses of Marx and the relations to Marx in this tradition of critical theory, but also on the uses of Hegel who has been decisive in the first and third generation of the Frankfurt school.

As already mentioned in the introduction, in its first generation, Frankfurt critical theory is a continuation of the Hegelian-Marxism of Lukács and Korsch. Like them, Horkheimer, Marcuse and Adorno consider that it is fully legitimate to read Hegel from a Marxian point of view. Furthermore, like Lukács and Korsch, they refer to Hegel as a means of re-evaluating the philosophical and critical moments of Marx's thought against the scientism and dogmatism of the Second and Third International. But the main figures of the first generation are also aware that with the development of psychoanalysis and the social sciences, it is no longer possible to read Marx and Hegel as before, and that only the use of these new knowledges makes it possible to understand how the social relationships of domination mold subjectivity and evoke social conflicts. What distinguishes their use of Hegel from that of Lukács and Korsch is that they draw on Hegel to transform Marx's social theory into an interdisciplinary research program[202] rather than simply reading Marx as a Hegelian. Hegel's processual ontology, identifying 'actuality' with 'reciprocal action', leads them to interpret the present from the point of view of its transformative tendencies while conceiving in a non-reductionist way, as a 'reciprocal action', the relationships between economics, psychoanalysis, and sociology of culture that are constitutive of the interdisciplinary research program.[203] The Hegelian conception of 'speculation' as an immanent critique of 'understanding', already mobilized by Hegel to regulate the relationship between the philosophy of nature and the positive sciences and by Marx to construct his critique of political economy, enable them to conceive of the critical theory of society as an immanent critique of sociology and psychoanalysis. This context explains why

201 And who remain one the the most interesting features of what can be called the 'late Marxism', see F. Jameson, *Late Marxism. Adorno or the persistence of dialectics*, London: Verso, 2006.

202 On this program, see H. Dubiel, *Wissenschaftsorganisation und politische Erfahrung*, Frankfurt: *Suhrkamp*, 1978.

203 On Hegel's processual ontology and its echoes in Marx and critical theory, see E. Renault, "Critical Theory and Processual Social Ontology."

Marx's critique of political economy could have become a model for critical theory. It provided a model of an interdisciplinary social theory elaborated via the immanent critique of social sciences, even if *Capital* is a critical examination of the concepts and principles of only one social science, namely, classical political economy. But it also provided a model for connecting social theory with political practice, since critique of political economy could be conceived of as a theoretical tool useful to help the communist movement tackle the problems it was confronted with. And finally, it was also the model of a theory aware of its belonging to its own time and to the clash of social interests that is a characteristic of the existing social order.

On the methodological level, Habermas, the major author of the second generation of Frankfurt critical theory, remained in continuity with this program,[204] as evidenced by his contributions to the 'Positivist dispute' in which Adorno and Popper confronted their opposite conceptions of rationality, science, and sociology.[205] But Habermas also considered that developments within the social sciences, psychoanalysis, and linguistics, as well as historical and political evolutions, justified reconstructing critical theory on another theoretical basis than that of Marx's critique of political economy. Critical theory then underwent a twofold pragmatist and communicative turn. According to Habermas, pragmatism makes it possible to think of the relation of knowledge and social interests in a more flexible sense than in Marx. It allows for the plurality of social interests to be taken into account and not only class interests. It also allows one to stop referring to the theme of the unity of theory and practice with reference to practice understood only as work and social struggles. It finally makes it possible to seek the norms of criticism in the normative expectations that structure social interactions while interpreting them from the point of view of a theory of social communication.[206] In this respect, the pragmatist turn is inseparable from a communicative turn which takes place in a theoretical conjuncture marked by different forms of a linguistic turn: Wittgenstein's philosophy of ordinary language, Gadamer's hermeneutics, and Apel's program of transcendental pragmatics. The result is a farewell to Hegel as well as to Marx. To Hegel insofar as it is Kant and not Hegel who solves the problem, unsolved in the first generation of the Frankfurt school, of the normative presuppositions of social criticism. To Marx, on the one hand, for social theory rejects

204 For such a presentation of Habermas, see R. Gueus, *The Idea of Critical Theory. Habermas and the Frankfort School*, Cambridge, UK: Cambridge University Press, 1981.

205 See T.W. Adorno, *The Positivist Dispute in German Sociology*, New York: Harper & Row, 1973.

206 J. Habermas, *Knowledge and Interests*.

the fundamental assumptions of the materialistic conception of history in order to reconstruct a normative social theory drawing notably on Parsons and Durkheim, and on the other hand, for this social theory is part of a theory of modernity, founded on Weber and Kant, and no longer of a theory of capitalism. Honneth, the main representative of the third generation of Frankfurt critical theory, inherits these pragmatist and communicative turns, while thinking of communication in terms of recognition. It is in reference to the pragmatism of Dewey and Mead that he tries to re-actualize Hegel's theory of recognition.[207]

The fact that Habermas made critical theory turn to pragmatism and communication produced irreversible effects. Just as after the first generation of critical theory it was no longer possible to belong to the tradition of critical theory without taking into account the social sciences and psychoanalysis, so too it became impossible after Habermas to embrace this tradition without taking into account the fact that different forms of communication and recognitive relationships are at work in social interactions. Hence the new possible readings of Hegel and Marx which wonder about the role played by recognition in their works.[208] On the other hand, in the same way that by building alliances with psychoanalysis and the social sciences, the first generation had somehow integrated their histories into that of critical theory, and had thereby made the latter tributary of the development of psychoanalysis and the social sciences, by building alliances with American pragmatism, which is another great theoretical-political tradition of the 20th and 21st centuries, the second and third generations have integrated the history of pragmatism in that of critical theory, while they were previously regarded as mutually hostile to each other. Hence the awareness of the affinities of pragmatism with the prehistory of critical theory, with Hegel on the one hand, which is known to have profoundly influenced Dewey, along with Marx on the other.[209]

If elements of continuity between Habermas and Honneth are therefore illustrative of the irreversible effects that have marked the history of critical theory, elements of discontinuity are no less significant. They essentially concern the fact that the latter has initially sought to reconnect with Hegel and Marx, and to do so in the manner of the first generation, that is to say, within the framework of a theory of society inspired by Marx more than by Hegel.

207 A. Honneth, *The Struggle for Recognition*.

208 On Marx and recognition, see the special issue of the journal *Ethical Theory and Moral Practice*, Volume 16, Issue 4, 2013.

209 On Dewey's relations to Marx, see E. Renault, "Dewey, Hook, and Mao: on some affinities between Marxism and pragmatism."

The fact that it is from a Marxian criticism of Habermas that Honneth elaborated the first program of his theory of recognition is attested by his early articles and should not be underestimated.[210] He convincingly pointed out that it was necessary to give again to social conflicts and structural social relations of domination the room they deserve in critical theory. The idea of a struggle for recognition was intended to highlight the specific normative potential of social conflicts and to think about it independently of the forms of rational justification that can be formed in the political public space, while insisting on the fact that this normative potential can no longer be expressed other than in social conflicts when relations of domination block access to the political public space. Honneth was then criticizing Habermas's conception of the political centrality of public deliberation from a Marxian point of view, namely, by contending that social life is structured by domination and conflict, and that in the context of structural social domination, public deliberations are hampered by ideological obstacles. In other words, Honneth was converting Marx's criticism of politics into a critique of the political centrality of public space. Honneth was also supporting the Marxian tradition of the politics of social conflicts while seeking in Hegel's theory of recognition a response to Habermas's critique of the normative deficit of Marx's conception of politics as class struggle. As struggles for recognition, according to Honneth, social conflicts are animated by principles of justice whose legitimacy can be philosophically established.

In the early Honneth, as in the first generation of critical theory, Marx was the main inspiration and Hegel was a means of reformulation of Marxian intuitions. But in the mature Honneth, in *Freedom's Right*[211] and other works, Hegel became the basis of social theory, while Marx is reduced to an operator of Hegel's reactualization, just like Dewey, with both of them playing a lesser role than Durkheim. The *Principles of the Philosophy of Law* define both the principles and the method of the theory of modern societies and of the immanent critique on which critical theory is to be grounded, and Marx is mainly a means of explaining how capitalism can divert modernity from the historical trajectory that would allow it to honor its promises.[212] The relationship between Marx and Hegel is thus reversed, and it is precisely this inversion that this book would have liked to have contributed to reverse again, by suggesting on the one

---

210 J.-P. Deranty, *Beyond Communication, op. cit.*

211 A. Honneth, *Freedom's Right: The Social Foundations of Democratic Life*, New York: Columbia University Press, 2014.

212 A. Honneth, "Hegel and Marx: A Reevaluation after a Century", https://www.youtube.com/watch?v=7b7dBIz_69E.

hand that social theory should conceive of societies as structured by relations of dominations and by conflicts between dominant and dominated groups, and by suggesting on the other hand that one should think of contemporary societies as structured primarily by the specificities of the capitalist mode of production and only secondarily by the rational promises of modernity. The coming decades will say if one of the trademarks of the fourth generation of critical theory, in case it becomes possible to use this term, will be the stronger connection of critical theory with Marx that this book would like to support.

References

Adorno, T.W., *Negative Dialectics*, New York: Routledge, 1973.

Adorno, T.W., *Aesthetic Theory*, New York: Continuum, 2004.

Adorno, T.W., *Philosophische Elemente einer Theorie der Gesellschaft*, Frankfurt: Suhrkamp, 2008.

Adorno, T.W., M. Horkheimer, *Dialectics of Enlightenment*, Stanford: Stanford University Press, 2002.

Adorno, T.W., and K. Popper, *The Positivist Dispute in German Sociology*, London: Heinemann, 1976.

Adorno, T.W., "Why Still Philosophy?", in *Critical Models: Interventions and Catchwords*, New York: Columbia University Press, 1998.

Adorno, T.W., "Marginalia to Theory and Praxis", in *Critical Models: Interventions and Catchwords*, New York: Columbia University Press, 1998.

Adorno, T.W., "Gesellschaft", in *Gesammelte Schriften*, volume 8, Frankfort: Suhrkamp, 2003.

Adorno, T.W., "Anmerkungen zum sozialen Konflikt heute", in *Gesammelte Schriften*, volume 8, Frankfort: Suhrkamp, 2003.

Althusser, L., *For Marx*, London: Verso, 1990.

Althusser, L., and E. Balibar, *Reading Capital*, London: Verso, 1997.

Althusser, L., *Lenin and Philosophy, and Other Essays*, New York: Monthly Review Press, 1972.

Arendt, H., *The Human Condition*, Chicago: The University of Chicago Press, 1998.

Arnold, D., "Gramsci and peasant subalternity in India", *The Journal of Peasant Studies*, Volume 11, Issue 4, 1984, 155–177.

Balibar, E., *The Philosophy of Marx*, London: Verso, 1995.

Bidet, J., *Foucault avec Marx*, Paris: La Fabrique, 2014.

Bidet-Mordrel, A., *Les Rapports sociaux de sexe*, Paris: PUF, 2010.

Bloch, E., *The Principle of Hope*, Cambridge, MA: MIT Press, 1986.

Bourdieu, P., *Pascalian Meditations*, Stanford: Stanford University Press, 2000.

Bowell, T., "Feminist Standpoint Theory", http://www.iep.utm.edu/fem-stan/.

Brecht, B., "Über eingreifendes Denken", in *Gesammelte Werke*, Frankfurt, Germany: Suhrkamp, 1967, 8.714–735.

Brudney, D., *Marx's Attempt to Leave Philosophy*, Cambridge, MA: Harvard University Press, 1998.

Burawoy, M., *Conversations with Bourdieu. The Johannesburg Moment*, Johannesburg: Wits University Press, 2012.

Butler, J., *The Psychic Life of Power*, Stanford: Stanford University Press, 1997.

Butler, J., *Giving an Account of Oneself*, New York: Fordham University Press, 2005.

Celikates, R., *Kritik als Soziale Praxis*, Frankfurt: Campus, 2009.

Cohen, G., *Karl Marx's Theory of History. A Defence*, Oxford: Clarendon Press, 2000.

Dardot, P., and C. Laval, *Marx, Prénom: Karl*, Paris: Gallimard, 2012.

Dejours, C., J.-P. Deranty, E. Renault, and N. Smith, *The Return of Work*, New York: Columbia University Press, 2018.

Deleuze, G., *Foucault*, London: Continuum, 2006.

Della Volpe, G., *Logic as a Positive Science*, London: NLB, 1980.

Deranty, J.-P., *Beyond Communication. A critical study of Honneth's social philosophy*, Leiden: Brill, 2009.

Derrida, J., *Specters of Marx: The State of the Debt, The Work of Mourning & the New International*, New York: Routledge, 1994.

Derrida, J., "Marx & Sons," in *Ghostly Demarcations: A Symposium on Jacques Derrida's Specters of Marx*, edited by M. Sprinker, London: Verso, 1999.

Dewey, J., *The Influence of Darwin on Philosophy and Other Essays*, New York: Henry Holt and Co., 1910.

Dewey, J., *Democracy and Education: An Introduction to the Philosophy of Education*, New York: Macmillan, 1916.

Dewey, J., *Reconstruction in Philosophy*, New York: Henry Holt and Co., 1920.

Dewey, J., *The Public and its Problems*, London: Allen & Unwin, 1926.

Dewey, J., "The Social as a Category," *Monist* 38 (April 1928), 161–177.

Dewey, J., *Experience and Nature*, New York: George Allen Unwin, 1929.

Dewey, J., *Art as Experience*, New York: Perigee Books, 2005.

Draper, H., *Marx's Theory of Revolution*, New York: Monthly Review Press, 2 Volumes, 1978.

Dubiel, H., *Wissenschaftsorganisation und politische Erfahrung*, Frankfurt: Suhrkamp, 1978.

Durkheim, E., *The Division of Labor in Society*, New York: Free Press, 1997.

Dumenil, G., and D. Lévy, *The Crisis of Neoliberalism*, Cambridge, MA: Harvard University Press, 2013.

Eagleton, T., *Ideology. An Introduction*, London: Verso, 1991.

Engels, F., *Ludwig Feuerbach and the End of Classical German Philosophy*, Moscow: Foreign Languages Pub. House, 1950.

Feenberg, A., *Philosophy of Praxis: Marx, Lukács and the Frankfurt School*, London: Verso, 2014.

Foster, J.B., *Marx's Ecology. Materialism and Nature*, New York: Monthly Review Press, 2000.

Foucault, M., "The Meshes of Power," in *Space, Knowledge and Power*: Foucault and geography / edited by Jeremy W. Crampton and Stuart Elden, Aldershot: Ashgate, 2007.

Foucault, M., *Discipline & Punish: The Birth of the Prison*, New York: Pantheon Books, 1977.

Foucault, M., "What is Enlightenment?" (1984), in *The Foucault Reader*, edited by P. Rabinow, New York: Pantheon, 1985.

Frank, M., *Der unendliche Mangel an Sein: Schellings Hegelkritik und die Anfänge der Marxschen Dialektik*, Munich: W. Fink Verlag, 1992.

Frank, M., "Schelling's Critique of Hegel and the Beginnings of Marxian Dialectics," *Idealistic Studies*, Volume 3, 2010: 251–268.

Frye, M., "Some Reflections on Separatism and Power", in *Feminist Social Thought: A Reader*, edited by D. Tietjens Meyers, New York: Routledge, 1997.

Goffman, E., "The Arrangement between the Sexes", *Theory and Society*, Volume 4, Number 3, 1977, 301–331.

Gould, C.C., *Marx's Social Ontology. Individuality and Community in Marx's Theory of Social Reality*, Cambridge, MA: MIT Press, 1975.

Gramsci, A., *Prison Notebooks*, New York: Columbia University Press, 2010.

Gueus, R., *The Idea of Critical Theory. Habermas and the Frankfort School*, Cambridge, UK: Cambridge University Press, 1981.

Habermas, J., *Knowledge and Human Interests*, Boston, MA: Beacon Press, 1971.

Habermas, J., "Towards a Reconstruction of Historical Materialism", *Theory and Society*, Volume 2, Number 3 (Autumn, 1975), 287–300.

Habermas, J., *The Theory of Communicative Action*, Boston, MA: Beacon Press, 1984.

Habermas, J., *The Philosophical Discourse of Modernity: Twelve Lectures*, Cambridge, MA: MIT Press, 1985.

Haber, S., *Penser le néocapitalisme. Vie, capital et aliénation*, Paris: Prairies ordinaires, 2013.

Haraway, D., "Situated Knowledge: The Science Question in Feminism and the Privilege of Partial Perspective", *Feminist Studies*, Volume 14, Issue 3, 1988, 575–599.

Haug, F., "Marx withing Feminism", http://www.friggahaug.inkrit.de/documents/marxinfem.pdf.

Hegel, G.W.F., *The Philosophy of Right*, Kitchener: Batoche, 2001.

Hegel, G.W.F., *Hegel's Logic. Being Part One of the Encyclopaedia of the Philosophical Sciences,* Oxford: Oxford University Press, 1975.

Honneth, A., *The Struggle for Recognition: The Moral Grammar of Social Conflicts*, trans. Joel Anderson, Cambridge, UK: Polity Press, 1995.

Honneth, A., *Reification. A New Look at an Old Idea*, Oxford: Oxford University Press, 2008.

Honneth, A., *Freedom's Right: The Social Foundations of Democratic Life*, New York: Columbia University Press, 2014.

Honneth, A., "The Possibility of a Disclosing Critique of Society: The Dialectic of Enlightenment in Light of Current Debates in Social Criticism", *Constellations*, Volume 7, Issue 1, 2000, 116–127.

Honneth, A., "Pathologies of the Social: The Past and Present of Social Philosophy", in *Disrespect: The Normative Foundations of Critical Theory*. Cambridge UK: Polity Press, 2007.

Honneth, A., "Die Moral im 'Kapital'. Versuch einer Korrektur der Marxschen Ökonomiekritik", in *Nach Marx, Philosophie, Kritik, Praxis*, edited by R. Jaeggi and D. Loïck, Frankfurt: Suhrkamp 2013.

Honneth, A., "Hegel and Marx: A Reevaluation after a Century", https://www.youtube.com/watch?v=7b7dBIz_69E.

Hook, S., *Towards the Understanding of Karl Marx, A Revolutionary Interpretation* (New York: John Day Co., 1933.

Horkheimer, M., "The State of Contemporary Social Philosophy and the Tasks of an Institute for Social Research", in *Critical Theory and Society: A Reader*, edited by. S.E. Bronner and D.M. Kellner, New York: Routledge, 1989.

Horkheimer, M., "Traditional and Critical Theory", in *Critical Theory: Selected Essays*, New York: Herder and Herder, 1972.

Jaeggi, R., *Alienation*, New York: Columbia University Press, 2014.

Jaeggi, R., "A Wide Concept of Economy: Economy as a Social Practice and the Critique of Capitalism", in *Critical Theory in Critical Times*, edited by P. Deutscher, New York: Columbia University Press, 2017.

Jameson, F., *Late Marxism. Adorno or the persistence of dialectics*, London: Verso, 2006.

Korsch, K., *Marxism and Philosophy*, New York: Monthly Review Press, 1971.

Korsch, K., *Karl Marx*, New York: Russell & Russell, 1963.

Labica, G., *Marxism and the Status of Philosophy*, Sussex, UK: Harvester Press, 1980.

Labriola, A., *Essays on the Materialistic Conception of History*, New York: Monthly Review Press, 1966.

Lenin, V., *Materialism and Empiriocriticism*, Peking: Foreign Languages Press, 1972.

Lindner, U., *Marx und die Philosophie*, Stuttgart: Schmetteling Verlag, 2013.

Lukács, G., *History and Class Consciousness: Studies in Marxist Dialectics*, Cambridge, MA: MIT Press, 1971.

Lukács, G., *Le Jeune Marx: son évolution philosophique de 1840 à 1844*, Paris: les Éd. de la Passion, 2002.

Macherey, P., *Hegel or Spinoza*, Minneapolis: University of Minnesota Press, 2011.

Marcuse, H., *Reason and Revolution: Hegel and the Rise of Social Theory*, New York: Humanities Press, 1955.

Marcuse, H., "Philosophy and Critical Theory", in *Negations: Essays in Critical Theory*, Boston: Beacon Press, 1968.

Marx, K., *Capital*, London: Penguin Classics, 3 volumes (quoted *Capital I, II, III*), 1990.

Marx, K., and F. Engels, *Collected Works*, London: Lawrence & Wishart, 50 volumes, 1975–2004.

Ollman, B., and T. Smith (eds), *Dialectics for the New Century*, Basingstoke, UK: Palgrave Macmillan, 2008.

Phelps, C., *Young Sidney Hook: Marxist and Pragmatist*, Ithaca, NY: Cornell University Press, 1997.

Plekhanov, G., *The Development of the Monist View of History*, Moscow: Foreign Languages Publishing House, 1956.

Postone, M., *Time, Labour, and Social Domination*, Cambridge, UK: Cambridge University Press, 1996.

Renault, E., *Marx et l'idée de critique*, Paris: Puf, 1995.

Renault, E., *Marx et la philosophie*, Paris: Puf, 2014.

Renault, E., *Connaître ce qui est. Enquête sur le présentisme hégélien*, Paris: Vrin, 2015.

Renault, E., "Dewey, Hook, and Mao: on some affinities between Marxism and pragmatism", http://www.cairn-int.info/article-E_AMX_054_0137--dewey-hook-mao-on-some-affinities.htm.

Renault, E., "The Naturalist Side of Hegel's Pragmatism", *Critical Horizons*, Volume 13, Issue 2, 2012, 244–274.

Renault, E., "Dewey's Relations to Hegel", *Contemporary Pragmatism*, Volume 13, Issue 3, 2016 219–241.

Renault, E., "Critical theory and processual social ontology", *Journal of Social Ontology*, Volume 2, Issue 1, 2016, 17–32.

Renault, E., "The Early Marx and Hegel: The Young Hegelian Mediation", forthcoming in *Reassessing Marx's Social and Political Philosophy*, edited by J. Kandiyali, New York: Routledge, forthcoming, 2018.

Renault, E., "Hegel, Marx, Presentism", in *From Marx to Hegel and Back Again*, edited by H. Kuch and V. Fareld, London: Bloomsbury, forthcoming, 2018.

Rorty, R., *Contingency, Irony and Solidarity*, Cambridge, UK: Cambridge University Press, 1989.

Sandkühler, H.-J., and R. de la Vega (eds), *Marxismus und Ethik: Texte zum neukantianischen Sozialismus*, Frankfurt: Suhrkamp, 1974.

Sartre, J.-P., *Critique of Dialectical Reason*, London: NLB, 1976.

Schatzki, T.R., K. Knorr Cetina, and E. von Savigny (eds), *The Practice Turn in Contemporary Theory*, New York: Routledge, 2001.

Sibertin-Blanc, G., *Politics and State. Deleuze and Guattari on Marx*, Cambridge, MA: MIT Press, 2016.

Weber, M., *The Protestant Ethic and the Spirit of Capitalism*, New York: Charles Scribner's Sons, 1950.

Weber, M., *Economy and Society*, Berkeley: California University Press, 1978.

Wendling, A.M., *Karl Marx on Technology and Alienation*, Basingstoke, UK: PalgraveMacmillan, 2009.

Wiggershaus, R., *The Frankfurt School: its history, theories and political significance*, Cambridge, MA: MIT Press, 1994.

Williams, R., *Marxism and Literature*, Oxford: Oxford University Press, 1977.

Wood, A., *Marx*, New York: Routledge, 2004.

Zurn, C., "Social Pathologies As Second-Order Disorders", in *Axel Honneth: Critical Essays. With a Reply by Axel Honneth*, edited by D. Petherbridge, Dordrecht: Brill, 2011.

www.ingramcontent.com/pod-product-compliance
Lightning Source LLC
Chambersburg PA
CBHW031331230926
51848CB00001B/194